POWER ENGLISH

BASIC LANGUAGE SKILLS FOR ADULTS

Dorothy Rubin

TRENTON STATE COLLEGE

CAMBRIDGE Adult Education
REGENTS/PRENTICE HALL
Englewood Cliffs, New Jersey 07632

PHOTO CREDITS

CHAPTER TWO: Teri Leigh Stratford

CHAPTER THREE: UPI/Bettmann Newsphotos

CHAPTER FOUR: Laima E. Druskis

CHAPTER FIVE: Teri Leigh Stratford

Editorial supervision: Timothy Foote
Production supervision: Alan Gold
Manufacturing buyer: Mike Woerner
Photo researcher: Page Poore

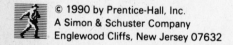 © 1990 by Prentice-Hall, Inc.
A Simon & Schuster Company
Englewood Cliffs, New Jersey 07632

Printed in the United States of America

10 9 8 7 6 5 4 3 2

ISBN 013–688490–3

Prentice-Hall International (UK) Limited, *London*
Prentice-Hall of Australia Pty. Limited, *Sydney*
Prentice-Hall Canada Inc., *Toronto*
Prentice-Hall Hispanoamericana, S.A., *Mexico*
Prentice-Hall of India Private Limited, *New Delhi*
Prentice-Hall of Japan, Inc., *Tokyo*
Simon & Schuster Asia Pte. Ltd., *Singapore*
Editora Prentice-Hall do Brasil, Ltda., *Rio de Janeiro*

CONTENTS

Power English: Basic Language Skills for Adults is a ten-book series dedicated to helping adults at the ABE level develop their skills in usage, sentence structure, mechanics, and composition. *Power English* consists of the locator test for the series, eight text/workbooks, and a series review book.

There are five chapters in each of the text/workbooks. The several lessons in each chapter cover a variety of writing skills. The comprehensive Chapter Reviews and Posttests in each book provide skill reinforcement. To facilitate diagnosis, there are Progress Charts for recording students' Chapter Review and Posttest performance. Answers are in a special section at the end of each book. The section can be left in the book so that students can check their own work, or since its pages are perforated, it can be removed.

Power English is comfortable for an adult whose reading level is between 4.0 and 8.0. Each lesson is a simple and concise presentation of a specific writing skill. In the instructional portion of a lesson, under the heading **Read the following** students study examples of a specific writing skill at work. Under **Did you notice?** they read short, clear explanations of the skill at hand. Because a typical lesson reinforces and expands upon skills taught in earlier lessons, a section called **Do you remember?** reviews pertinent rules and concepts previously presented. The **Try it out** portion of a lesson provides exercise for applying and practicing the new and reviewed skills.

Power English encourages the rapid and enjoyable acquisition of fundamental writing skills. The program is based on sound learning principles and is devised to keep the student actively engaged throughout. It incorporates the following:

- self-pacing
- graduated levels of difficulty
- distributed practice
- immediate feedback
- overlearning
- teaching of generalizations where applicable
- selections based on adult interests

Power English is founded on the principle of overlearning, which fosters enduring retention of information and skills. Overlearning occurs when students continue practicing a skill even after they think they have learned it. In every chapter and book in the *Power English* series, through a variety of formats, students exercise skills they have learned in previous chapters and books.

The structure of the *Power English* series makes it versatile. It can be used in conventional classroom settings, in tutorial situations and clinics, or by students who work independently.

CAPITALIZING (MOVIE AND TV SHOW TITLES)

Read the following:

MOVIES	TELEVISION SHOWS
<u>A Man for All Seasons</u>	"Golden Girls"
<u>Rocky</u>	"The Cosby Show"

Did you notice?

Most words in the titles of movies and television shows begin with capital letters.

Movie titles are underlined.

Quotations marks (" ") go around the titles of television shows.

Do you remember?

Most words in book titles begin with capital letters.

Book titles are underlined.

Try it out.

Write each sentence over correctly.

1. my favorite movie is still <u>casablanca</u> with humphrey bogart.

   _____

2. johnny carson is the host of "the tonight show" on nbc.

   _____

3. ronald reagan was in the film <u>king's row</u> .

   _____

4. like many books, <u>from here to eternity</u> became a movie.

   _____

5. in march i read george orwell's <u>animal farm</u> again.

   _____

STOP CHECK ANSWERS ON PAGE 137.

2

SINGULAR AND PLURAL SUBJECTS

Read the following:

SINGULAR SUBJECTS	PLURAL SUBJECTS
The <u>ape</u> climbs the tree.	The <u>apes</u> climb the tree.
My <u>husband</u> is a lawyer.	My <u>husband</u> and <u>I</u> are lawyers.
The <u>window</u> looks dirty.	The <u>windows</u> look dirty.
<u>He</u> trusts him.	<u>They</u> trust him.

Do you remember?

There is at least one noun or pronoun in the complete subject of a sentence. When the noun or pronoun in a complete subject names one person or thing, the subject of the sentence is singular.

The subject of a sentence is plural when it names more than one person or thing.

The subject of a sentence is plural when it contains two or more nouns or pronouns.

Try it out.

Underline the nouns and pronouns in the complete subjects of each of the following sentences. Write **S** in the blank if the subject of the sentence is singular. Write **P** in the blank if the subject of the sentence is plural.

1. Many <u>people</u> get divorced today. _____P_____

2. My <u>brother</u> just got divorced. _____S_____

3. <u>Bill</u> and <u>I</u> will never get a divorce. _____P_____

4. The <u>idea</u> sounds strange to me. _____S_____

5. A <u>divorce</u> hurts many people. _____S_____

6. My <u>parents</u> have been married a long time. _____P_____

7. <u>Frank</u> and <u>Kathy</u> are divorced now. _____P_____

8. <u>They</u> have two children. _____P_____

9. Their <u>children</u> are very unhappy. _____P_____

10. <u>It</u> is too bad about the divorce. _____S_____

STOP CHECK ANSWERS ON PAGE 137.

COMBINING SENTENCES

Read the following:

In these sentences, the predicates are similar.

Stan likes his job a lot.
Terry likes his job a lot.
I like my job a lot.

Now read the following:

This sentence combines those three sentences.

Stan, Terry, and I like our jobs a lot.

Did you notice?

The subject is plural in the combined sentence: **Stan, Terry, and I**.
The plural subject requires a plural verb: **like**.
The words **our jobs** are used because the long sentence talks about three people's jobs.

Do you remember?

In the long sentence, commas and the word **and** are used to join the subjects from the short sentences.
The words **a lot** are used only once in the long sentence.

Try it out.

Write one sentence that combines the sentences in each set.

1. Marie is eating her breakfast.
   José is eating his breakfast.
   Mike is eating his breakfast.

   M, J, and mike are eating their breakfasts

   _____

2. Charles goes to his club on Saturdays.
   Jim goes to his club on Saturdays.
   I go to my club on Saturdays.

   Char, Jim, and I go to our club on Saturdays

   _____

GO ON TO THE NEXT PAGE

3. My father likes his gift.
My mother likes her gift.
I like my gift.

My father, my mother, and I like our Gifts.

4. George rides his bike to work every day.
Pat rides her bike to work every day.
Kim rides her bike to work every day.

G, Pat, and Kim ride their bikes to work every day.
G, P, K ride their bikes every day

5. My bird plays with its toy.
My cat plays with its toy.

My bird and cat play with their toys.
my bird and cat play w/ their toys

COMBINING SENTENCES

Read the following:

In these sentences, the predicates are similar.
Kenji has his ticket already.
Maria has her ticket already.
Luiz has his ticket already.

Now read the following:

This sentences combines those three sentences.
Kenji, Maria, and Luiz have their tickets already.

Did you notice?

The subject is plural in the combined sentence: **Kenji, Maria, and Luiz**.
The plural subject requires a plural verb: **have**.
The words **their tickets** are used because the long sentence talks about three people's tickets.

Do you remember?

In the long sentence, commas and the word **and** are used to join the subjects from the short sentences.
The word **already** is used only once in the long sentence.

Try it out.

Write one sentence that combines all the sentences in each set.

1. Grant is starting his new job today.
   Keung is starting his new job today.
   Barney is starting his new job today.

   G, K, and Barney are starting their new job today
   G, K, B, are start her

2. Teresa uses her credit card too much.
   Ben uses his credit card too much.

   T and ben use their c.c too much
   Ter, B. use thir c.

GO ON TO THE NEXT PAGE

3. The cat drinks milk every day.
   Wayne drinks milk every day.
   Jessie drinks milk every day.

   The cat, Wayne, and Jessie drink milk every day.

   The cat, Way & Jes dr

4. Henri put his house on the market today.
   Pina put her house on the market today.
   Ali put his house on the market today.

   H, Pina and Ali put his their house on the market today

5. Eleni buys her groceries every day.
   Ann buys her groceries every day.
   Diego buys his groceries every day.

   E, Ann and Diego buy their groceries. every day

STOP CHECK ANSWERS ON PAGE 137.

END MARKS (PUNCTUATION)

Read the following:
> How romantic that is!
> Who is she?
> Don't go yet.
> Help!
> She looks pretty today.

Do you remember?
A statement ends with a period (.).
A question ends with a question mark **(?)**.
A sentence that shows strong feeling ends with an exclamation point **(!)**.
A command usually ends with a period (.).
If a command shows strong feeling, it ends with an exclamation point (!).
A command usually has the unstated subject **you**.

Did you know?
End marks can also be called **end punctuation**.

Try it out.
Put the proper end mark at the end of each sentence.

1. Whose dog is that ?

2. That is incredible news |

3. Who is going to the movies ?

4. Please move

5. Grab that person

6. He looks happy

7. You look fantastic !

8. Slow down when you come to curves

9. Please share these

10. How many people will be here today

STOP CHECK ANSWERS ON PAGE 137.

PRONOUNS AND WHAT THEY REFER TO

Read the following:

My son likes his job.
Herb and Ying love their new house.
My dog wags its tail a lot.

Did you notice?

The pronoun **his** refers to the noun **son**.
The noun **son** comes before the pronoun **his**.
The pronoun **their** refers to the nouns **Herb** and **Ying**.
The nouns **Herb** and **Ying** come before the pronoun **their**.
The pronoun **its** refers to the noun **dog**.
The noun **dog** comes before the pronoun **its**.

Try it out.

Fill in each blank with the correct pronoun.

1. The funny girl clown stood on _____ her _____ head.

2. The little boy gave _____ his _____ balloon to the clown.

3. Carmen and Sally put _____ their _____ coats in the closet.

4. I need to fix _____ my _____ car.

5. The small white cat ate _____ its _____ food.

6. The tree shook off _____ its _____ leaves.

7. We need _____ Our _____ sleep.

8. The children took _____ their _____ pet for a walk.

9. Henri works on _____ his _____ computer.

10. Dave and Pauline brought _____ their _____ child to the party.

STOP CHECK ANSWERS ON PAGE 137.

9

ADJECTIVES

Try it out.

Fill in each blank with the correct adjective.

1. Is that the _____*Best*_____ you can do? (**good, better,** or **best**)

2. He has _____*many*_____ friends. (**many, more,** or **most**)

3. George has a _____*worse*_____ cold than you. (**bad, worse,** or **worst**)

4. That is the _____*worst*_____ thing I have ever seen. (**bad, worse,** or **worst**)

5. You seem _____*better*_____ today than yesterday. (**good, better,** or **best**)

6. Ana has the _____*most*_____ votes of all. (**many, more,** or **most**)

7. Tran wrote the _____*Best*_____ paper in the class. (**good, better,** or **best**)

8. Giselle is _____*good*_____ at everything she does. (**good, better,** or **best**)

9. My cat has lived _____*more*_____ years than yours. (**many, more,** or **most**)

10. This is the _____*Best*_____ night of my life. (**good, better,** or **best**)

STOP CHECK ANSWERS ON PAGE 137.

REGULAR AND IRREGULAR VERBS

Read the following:

		PRESENT	PAST	FUTURE
Regular Verbs	{	I work.	I worke_d_.	I will work.
		I preach.	I preache_d_.	I will preach.
		I hate.	I hate_d_.	I will hate.
Irregular Verbs	{	I forget.	I <u>forgot</u>.	I will forget.
		I go.	I <u>went</u>.	I will go.
		I think.	I <u>thought</u>.	I will think.

Did you notice?

There are two kinds of verbs: **regular** and **irregular**.
Regular verbs end with **d** or **ed** in past time.
Irregular verbs have special forms to show past time.
There are no differences in the ways regular and irregular verbs show present or future time.

Try it out.

At the end of each sentence is a regular or an irregular verb. Complete each sentence by writing the form of the verb that shows past time in the blank.

1. They _____*ed*_____ football yesterday. (**play**—regular)

2. She _____*ed*_____ at the loud noise. (**jump**—regular)

3. I _____*went*_____ to work early this morning. (**go**—irregular)

4. They _____*did*_____ better last year. (**do**—irregular)

5. He finally _____*learnt*_____ his lesson. (**learn**—regular)

6. Violet's anger _____*ate*_____ away at her all day. (**eat**—irregular)

7. Nothing _____*ed*_____ her get over it. (**help**—regular)

8. She _____*pped*_____ holding it in. (**stop**—regular)

9. She _____*had*_____ a fit. (**have**—irregular)

10. Then she _____*began*_____ to feel calmer. (**begin**—irregular)

STOP CHECK ANSWERS ON PAGE 137.

11

ADVERBS

Read the following:

The underlined words in the following sentences are adverbs.

Fung and I work <u>hard</u>.

Juan types <u>slowly</u>.

Now read the following:

Fung and I work <u>harder</u> than the others.

Juan types <u>more slowly</u> than anyone I know.

Did you notice?

The words **harder** and **more slowly** compare the action of one person to the action of another.

Many adverbs end with **er** when they compare two actions.

The word **more** goes before other adverbs when they compare two actions.

But notice this:

Some adverbs can show comparison either way.

We study <u>oftener</u> than they do.

We study <u>more often</u> than they do.

Try it out.

In the blank, write the comparing form of the adverb correctly. Add the word **more** or the **er** ending.

1. My friend swims _____*faster*_____ than you. (**fast**)

2. The man spoke _____*more harshly*_____ than I expected. (**harshly**)

3. The crowd of people acted _____*more*_____ than they should have. (**rudely**)

4. Anna watched the child _____*more*_____ than his mother did. (**carefully**)

5. Peter buys things _____*more*_____ than his wife. (**cheaply**)

6. Adela cried _____*louder*_____ than the bride's mother at the wedding. (**loud**)

7. The cat chases mice _____*more often*_____ than my other cat. (**often**)

8. This ribbon's color shines _____ than that ribbon's. (**brightly**)

9. Jim's girlfriend speaks _____ than Jim. (**rapidly**)

10. She usually tries _____*harder*_____ than you. (**hard**)

STOP CHECK ANSWERS ON PAGE 137.

ADVERBS

Read the following:

The underlined words in the following sentences are adverbs.

Sharon usually arrives <u>early</u>.

Ricardo works <u>hard</u>.

Samuel writes <u>often</u>.

Now read the following:

Sharon usually arrives the <u>earliest</u>.

Ricardo usually works the <u>hardest</u>.

Samuel writes the <u>oftenest</u>.

Samuel writes the <u>most often</u>.

Did you notice?

The words **earliest**, **hardest**, **oftenest**, and **most often** compare the action of one person to the actions of others.

Many adverbs end with **est** when they compare more than two actions.

The word **most** goes before other adverbs when they compare more than two actions.

Some adverbs, like **often**, can show comparison either way.

Try it out.

In the blank, write the comparing form of the adverb correctly. Add the word **most** or the **est** ending.

1. She spoke the _____ of all the people. (**loud**)

2. My boat traveled the ___slowest___ of all. (**slowly**)

3. His brother acted the ___craziest___ of anyone I know. (**crazy**)

4. Lin spoke the ___longest___ of all the speakers. (**long**)

5. Angela drove the ___most___ of all the drivers. (**carefully**)

6. Francis yelled the ___most___ of all of us. (**furiously**)

7. This mouse ate the cheese the ___most___ _quickest_. (**quickly**)

8. Neda spoke the ___clearest___ about the topic. (**clearly**)

9. That man acts the ___rudest___ of all the people I have met. (**rude**)

10. This golfer swings the ___steadiest___ of all the golfers here. (**steady**)

STOP CHECK ANSWERS ON PAGE 138.

SHOWING OWNERSHIP OR BELONGING TO (POSSESSION)

Read the following:

The underlined words in these sentences show singular possession.

My <u>grandfather's</u> nose is red.

<u>James's</u> nose is broken.

Now read the following:

The underlined words in these sentences show plural possession.

My <u>parents'</u> home is in Virginia.

Both <u>Charleses'</u> cars are in the shop.

Our <u>children's</u> home is in Hawaii.

Do you remember?

For singular nouns, possession is shown with this mark (') + **s**.

When a plural noun ends with **s**, possession is shown by adding this mark (') after the **s**.

Some plural nouns, like **children**, do not end with **s**.

For such plural nouns, ownership is shown by adding this mark (') + **s**.

Try it out.

Fill in each blank with the noun so that it shows possession correctly.

1. My _____ voice is too loud. (**boss**)

2. _____ car is red. (**Andrew**)

3. The _____ paint is peeling. (**shelves**)

4. _____ class is going on a picnic. (**Mrs. Brown**)

5. His _____ name is Bobby. (**father**)

6. My _____ pictures are cute. (**baby**)

7. The _____ club invited me. (**women**)

8. _____ shirt needs ironing. (**Jeff**)

9. The _____ parents are here. (**children**)

10. The _____ color is not right. (**peaches**)

STOP CHECK ANSWERS ON PAGE 138.

WRITING AN INVITATION

Read the following:

```
                                    September 8, 1990

Dear Tony and Angie,

    We are celebrating our tenth wedding anniversary and
would like you to join us. The party will be at our house
on Saturday night, September 20. Dress informally and come
prepared to eat a lot.
    Please phone to let us know if you can make it. Our
phone number is (609) 555-5748.
    I am enclosing a map to help you get to our new home at
131 Hardy street.

                                    Fondly,

                                    Art and Dot
```

Do you remember?

In a friendly letter, commas are used in the date and after the greeting and the closing.

The first word in the greeting and in the closing is capitalized.

Names in the greeting and closing are capitalized.

Paragraphs are indented, but the left edge of the body is in line with the greeting.

An invitation gives the day, date, time, place, and purpose of the party.

GO ON TO THE NEXT PAGE

Try it out.

Write a letter to invite a couple to a party at your house.

STOP CHECK SAMPLE INVITATION ON PAGE 138.

SPELLING

Try it out.
Look at each word. Then cover it and write it in the blank. Check your spelling.
Finally, write a sentence using the word.

1. until   _until_

_____

2. loose   _loose_

_____

3. through   _through_

_____

4. please   _Please_

_____

5. quiet   _quiet_

_____

STOP   CHECK SAMPLE ANSWERS ON PAGE 138.

ALPHABETIZING (USING THE DICTIONARY)

Do you remember?

A dictionary has guide words at the top of each page.
The guide words tell which are the first and last words on that page.
All words between the two guide words are on that page in alphabetical order.

Read the following:

Here is a sample of the guide words at the top of a dictionary page.

drain   eaten

Try it out.

Use the guide words **drain** and **eaten** to answer these questions. Write **Yes** or **No** in each blank.

1. Is the word **duck** on this page? _____

2. Is the word **ear** on this page? _____

3. Is the word **drag** on this page? _____

4. Is the word **early** on this page? _____

5. Is the word **easy** on this page? _____

6. Is the word **dream** on this page? _____

7. Is the word **dreary** on this page? _____

8. Is the word **eating** on this page? _____

9. Is the word **draw** on this page? _____

10. Is the word **drape** on this page? _____

STOP   CHECK ANSWERS ON PAGE 138.

CAPITALIZING (MOVIE AND TV SHOW TITLES)

Write each sentence over correctly.

1. the color purple with whoopie goldberg and oprah winfrey is an excellent
   movie that takes place in the south.

   _____

   _____

2. the film fatal attraction is a thrilling movie.

   _____

   _____

3. empire of the sun is a film about the japanese in shanghai in world war II.

   _____

   _____

4. cry freedom is a film based on the life of stephen biko, a black activist.

   _____

   _____

5. the old "father knows best" with robert young was a family television show.

   _____

   _____

SINGULAR AND PLURAL SUBJECTS

Underline the nouns and pronouns in the complete subjects of each of the
following sentences. Write **S** in the blank if the subject of the sentence is
singular. Write **P** in the blank if the subject of the sentence is plural.

1. The two men rushed into the apartment and started shooting. _P_

2. They were crazy with hate and revenge. _P_

3. Their sister and younger brother had just been killed by the drug dealer. _P_

4. The drug dealer had sold them impure drugs. _S_

5. The brothers took justice into their own hands and became murderers. _P_

GO ON TO THE NEXT PAGE

COMBINING SENTENCES

Write one sentence that combines the sentences in each set.

1. James is taking his vacation soon.
   Clara is taking her vacation soon.
   Felipe is taking his vacation soon.

   _____

   _____

2. The cat is eating now.
   The dog is eating now.
   The hamster is eating now.

   _____

   _____

3. Jane loves her new apartment.
   Brigitte loves her new apartment.
   I love my new apartment.

   _____

   _____

4. Larry enjoys his job.
   Betty enjoys her job.

   _____

5. Franco is working on his own.
   Michel is working on his own.
   Antonio is working on his own.

   _____

   _____

END MARKS (PUNCTUATION)

Put the proper end mark at the end of each sentence.

1. Are you sure he will be there

2. No, I can't go

3. This is really great

4. How much should I pay for it

5. I like her a lot

GO ON TO THE NEXT PAGE

PRONOUNS AND WHAT THEY REFER TO

Fill in each blank with the correct pronoun.

1. My mother makes _____ own delicious meat sauces.

2. My parents are celebrating _____ thirtieth wedding anniversary.

3. Hossein and I left _____ tools at work.

4. I want _____ own credit card.

5. The dog hurt _____ eye.

ADJECTIVES

Fill in each blank with the correct adjective.

1. He is the _____ person for the job. (**good, better,** or **best**)

2. He is _____ than she. (**good, better,** or **best**)

3. He is the _____ player I have seen yet. (**bad, worse,** or **worst**)

4. Julio makes _____ money than his brother. (**many, more,** or **most**)

5. Colette did the _____ work yesterday. (**many, more,** or **most**)

REGULAR AND IRREGULAR VERBS

At the end of each sentence is a regular or an irregular verb. Complete each sentence by writing the form of the verb that shows past time in the blank.

1. I _____ too much beer last night. (**drink**—irregular)

2. We _____ pool until four in the morning. (**play**—regular)

3. I _____ better than I usually do. (**do**—irregular)

4. Some people _____ near the bar. (**dance**—regular)

5. By midnight we all _____ each other. (**know**—irregular)

6. Several people _____ drunk. (**get**—irregular)

7. George _____ a few people home. (**help**—regular)

8. He _____ to make three trips. (**have**—irregular)

9. He _____ all around town. (**go**—irregular)

10. It _____ very kind of him. (**is**—irregular)

GO ON TO THE NEXT PAGE

ADVERBS

In the blank, write the comparing form of the adverb correctly. Add the word **more** or **most**, or the **er** or **est** ending.

1. The truck driver drives _____ than you. **(carefully)**

2. Ben speaks _____ than Fred. **(rapidly)**

3. My father laughs the _____. **(loud)**

4. The deer moved the _____ of the animals. **(swiftly)**

5. The mayor then spoke _____ than before. **(angrily)**

SHOWING OWNERSHIP OR BELONGING TO (POSSESSION)

Fill in each blank with the noun so that it shows possession correctly.

1. _____ sister is very pretty. **(Hideo)**

2. _____ store is doing well. **(Claude)**

3. My _____ mother is visiting today. **(wife)**

4. The _____ club is not open to men. **(women)**

5. Both _____ jobs are at the school. **(Pappases)**

WRITING AN INVITATION

Write a letter to invite someone to an anniversary party.

_____

_____

_____

_____

_____

_____

_____

_____

_____

GO ON TO THE NEXT PAGE

SPELLING

Use each of the following words in a sentence.

1. until

   _____

2. loose

   _____

3. through

   _____

4. please

   _____

5. quiet

   _____

ALPHABETIZING (USING THE DICTIONARY)

Use the guide words **broom** and **bump** to answer the questions. Write **Yes** or **No** in each blank.

1. Is the word **brown** on this page?   _____
2. Is the word **brother** on this page?   _____
3. Is the word **burn** on this page?   _____
4. Is the word **broil** on this page?   _____
5. Is the word **but** on this page?   _____

STOP   CHECK ANSWERS BEGINNING ON PAGE 138.

Count how many items you answered correctly in each **Section** of the Chapter One Review. Write your score per section in the **My Scores** column. If all of your section scores are as high as the **Good Scores**, go on to Chapter Two. If any of your section scores are lower than the **Good Scores**, study the lessons on the assigned **Review Pages** again before you go on to Chapter Two.

Section	Good Scores	My Scores	Review Pages
Capitalizing (Movie and TV Show Titles)	4 or 5		2
Singular and Plural Subjects	4 or 5		3
Combining Sentences	4 or 5		4–7
End Marks (Punctuation)	4 or 5		8
Pronouns and What They Refer To	4 or 5		9
Adjectives	4 or 5		10
Regular and Irregular Verbs	8, 9, or 10		11
Adverbs	4 or 5		12–13
Showing Ownership or Belonging To (Possession)	4 or 5		14
Writing an Invitation	A correct letter		15–16
Spelling	4 or 5		17
Alphabetizing (Using the Dictionary)	4 or 5		18

CHAPTER TWO

CAPITALIZING (NAMES OF COMPANIES)

Read the following:

ABC Chemical Company   Ace Plumbers   Drake Electronics

Did you notice?

Words in the <u>names of companies</u> begin with capital letters.

Try it out.

Rewrite each sentence correctly.

1. mr. grant works for the abc motor company in maine.

   Mr. Grank   ABC Motor Company   Maine

2. george, frank, and i work for a computer company called computer world.

   G, F, I   Computer World

3. i am a carpenter and work for atlas building company.

   I   Atlas Building Company.

4. nick and tony are waiters at club happiness.

   N + T   Club Happiness

5. the banker at national bank lives in oakland, california.

6. a new french cook starts work at the paradise restaurant in may.

7. aunt sara and uncle bill own the capital laundry service.

8. miss sanchez quit her job at the corbett ford company.

9. i brought my car to the fix everything garage on main street.

10. mr. and mrs. holly started work at the limited express company last tuesday.

STOP   CHECK ANSWERS ON PAGE 139.

26

AGREEMENT OF SUBJECT AND VERB

Read the following:

Mary is at school.
Carl needs my help.
Joe is very small.

Now read the following:

Mary's children are at school.
Carl's parents need my help.
Joe's cat is very small.

Did you notice?

A verb agrees with its subject.
The underlined word in each sentence is the noun in the complete subject that controls the verb.
When that noun is singular, the verb is also singular.
When that noun is plural, the verb is also plural.
Nouns that show possession do not control verbs.

Try it out.

Underline the verb that is correct for each sentence.

1. The man's pets (**are** or **is**) at his farm.

2. The children's sandbox (**are** or **is**) small.

3. Lin's friends (**visit** or **visits**) her often.

4. Daniel's face (**are** or **is**) very red.

5. Mr. and Mrs. Montoya's dog (**bark** or **barks**) all night long.

6. Beto and Diana's house (**has** or **have**) many bathrooms.

7. Junko's lips (**are** or **is**) chapped.

8. Nina's earrings (**look** or **looks**) nice.

9. My cousins' house (**needs** or **need**) a coat of paint.

10. Jorge's parrots (**talk** or **talks**) all the time.

CHECK ANSWERS ON PAGE 139.

COMBINING SENTENCES

Read the following:

Mildred likes people.
Mildred visits her friends often.

Now read the following:

Mildred likes people, and she visits her friends often.

Did you notice?

The two short sentences about Mildred are combined in the long sentence.
A comma (,) and the word **and** are used to combine the sentences.
The pronoun **she** is used instead of **Mildred** in the second part of the longer
sentence.

Try it out.

Write one sentence that combines the two in each of the following pairs. Follow
the model above.

1. Mallory plays the piano well, *and she*
   Mallory performs for his friends.

   _____

2. Keith is retired, *and he*
   Keith stays home most of the time.

   _____

3. Mildred works nine months a year, *and she*
   Mildred has the summer off.

   _____

4. Their house is in Brooklyn, *and it is*
   Their house is rather old.

   _____

5. The park is nearby, *and it*
   The park is often crowded with people.

   _____

STOP CHECK ANSWERS ON PAGE 139.

COMBINING SENTENCES

Read the following:

Frank has money problems.
Frank needs to find a job.

Now read the following:

Frank has money problems <u>and</u> needs to find a job.

Did you notice?

The two short sentences about Frank are combined in the long sentence.
The noun **Frank**, which is the subject, is written only once in the longer sentence.
The word **and** is used to combine the sentences.
No comma (,) is used.

Try it out.

Write one sentence that combines the two in each of the following pairs. Follow the model above.

1. She makes a lot of money. and
   ~~She~~ goes on many free trips.

   _____

2. David is running for City Council. and
   ~~David~~ needs a lot of votes to win.

   _____

3. The present councilman wants to stay in office. and
   The present councilman is <u>campaigning</u>.

   _____

4. The voters want a change. and
   The voters need <u>someone they can trust</u>.

   _____

5. The election is in three days. and
   The election <u>promises to be very exciting</u>.

   _____

STOP CHECK ANSWERS ON PAGE 139.

COMBINING SENTENCES

Read the following:

My father earns a good salary.
My father takes good care of us.

Now read the following:

My father earns a good salary, and he takes good care of us.
My father earns a good salary and takes good care of us.

Did you notice?

The two short sentences about my father are combined in two different ways.

The first way uses a comma (,) and the words **and** and **he** in the longer sentence.

The second sentence uses only the word **and**. The words **my father** are written only once.

Try it out.

Combine each pair of sentences in two different ways, following the models above. Write two different sentences for each pair.

1. Fumiko has a new job.
   Fumiko is moving to Chicago.

   _____

   _____

2. Mrs. Wong just bought a new car.
   Mrs. Wong is going away on vacation.

   _____

   _____

3. Ms. Davis plays tennis.
   Ms. Davis wins many matches.

   _____

   _____

GO ON TO THE NEXT PAGE

4. Isabel wants to be an actress.
   Isabel is going to acting school.

   _____

   _____

5. Scott's house is not too large.
   Scott's house needs many repairs.

   _____

   _____

STOP CHECK ANSWERS ON PAGE 140.

THE PRONOUNS ANYONE, EVERYONE, NO ONE, AND SOMEONE

Read the following:

<u>Anyone</u> is welcome here.
<u>Everyone</u> is invited to the party.
<u>No one</u> has taken my coat.
<u>Someone</u> has my book.

Did you notice?

The underlined words in the sentences above are pronouns.
They can stand for any person.
The words **anyone**, **everyone**, **no one**, and **someone** are singular, just as the word **one** is singular.
They go with singular verbs, such as **is** and **has**.
No one is written with two words.

Try it out.

Draw a line under the verb that is correct for the sentence.

1. Someone always (**put** or **puts**) an apple on my desk.

2. Anyone (**has** or **have**) a right to say that.

3. Someone (**play** or **plays**) the piano late at night.

4. Everyone (**want** or **wants**) me to stay.

5. Someone (**cry** or **cries**) every morning in the next room.

6. No one (**is** or **are**) happy here.

7. Everyone (**is** or **are**) nice to me.

8. Someone (**feel** or **feels**) sorry for him.

9. Everyone (**like** or **likes**) her.

10. No one (**remember** or **remembers**) that murder.

STOP   CHECK ANSWERS ON PAGE 140.

PRONOUNS (SHOWING OWNERSHIP OR BELONGING TO)

Read the following:

This apartment is <u>mine</u>.   This is <u>my</u> apartment.
This apartment is <u>yours</u>.   This is <u>your</u> apartment.
This apartment is <u>his</u>.   This is <u>his</u> apartment.
This apartment is <u>hers</u>.   This is <u>her</u> apartment.
This apartment is <u>its</u>.   This is <u>its</u> apartment.
This apartment is <u>ours</u>.   This is <u>our</u> apartment.
This apartment is <u>theirs</u>.   This is <u>their</u> apartment.

Do you remember?

These pronouns show ownership:

mine	yours	his	hers	its	ours	theirs
my	your	his	her	its	our	their

The pronouns do not need this mark (').

Try it out.

Fill in each blank correctly with a pronoun that shows ownership.

1. This is my room.

   This room is _____ .

2. This is my cat's coat.

   This is _____ coat.

3. These are my friends' books.

   These are _____ books.

   These books are _____ .

4. Helen's hair is gray.

   _____ hair is gray.

5. Victor's wallet is lost.

   _____ wallet is lost.

GO ON TO THE NEXT PAGE

6. That crook stole Viola's money.

That crook stole _____ money.

7. That is Marianne's sandwich.

That sandwich is _____ .

That is _____ sandwich.

8. My aunt's child is my cousin.

_____ child is my cousin.

9. Mr. Chandra's job is very important.

_____ job is very important.

10. The dog's tail was hurt.

_____ tail was hurt.

STOP CHECK ANSWERS ON PAGE 140.

REGULAR AND IRREGULAR VERBS

Read the following:

	PRESENT	PAST	FUTURE
Regular Verbs	Mike cries.	Mike cried.	Mike will cry.
	They dance.	They danced.	They will dance.
	He and I study.	He and I studied.	He and I will study.
Irregular Verbs	Mike eats.	Mike ate.	Mike will eat.
	They sit.	They sat.	They will sit.
	He and I sleep.	He and I slept.	He and I will sleep.

Do you remember?

Regular verbs end with **d** or **ed** in past time.

When a verb ends with a consonant + **y**, the **y** is changed to **i** before **ed** is added to show past time, as in **studied**.

Irregular verbs have special forms to show past time.

There are no differences in the ways regular and irregular verbs show present or future time.

Try it out.

In the blank, write the form of each verb that shows past time.

REGULAR VERBS

1. try _____
2. train _____
3. show _____
4. spy _____
5. wash _____

IRREGULAR VERBS

6. run _____
7. get _____
8. know _____
9. drink _____
10. go _____

STOP CHECK ANSWERS ON PAGE 140.

THE WORDS *WELL, BETTER,* AND *BEST*

Read the following:

well   better   best

Did you know?

The word **well** has special forms to show comparison.
Better is used to compare two persons, things, or actions.
Best is used to compare more than two persons, things, or actions.

Do you remember?

Well is an adverb when it describes how something is done.
Well is an adjective when it refers to someone's health.
   I feel **well**.
   They are feeling **well** today.

Try it out.

Fill in each blank with the correct form of the word **well**.

1. The runners ran _____ in this race than in the last.

2. I'm happy to say that Jim is feeling _____ today than yesterday.

3. Donna sings the _____ of all.

4. Tara feels _____ .

5. The clowns acted their _____ at this show.

6. Mino drove the _____ in the race.

7. Tom and Jane slept _____ in this room than in the other.

8. Andrew played basketball the _____ today.

9. Sara works _____ in a warm place than in a cold one.

10. The boss speaks _____ of you.

STOP   CHECK ANSWERS ON PAGE 140.

36

SHOWING OWNERSHIP OR BELONGING TO (POSSESSION)

Read the following:

My <u>friend's</u> child is nice.
My <u>friends'</u> children are nice.

His <u>wife's</u> apron is wet.
Their <u>wives'</u> aprons are wet.

The <u>goose's</u> egg is large.
The <u>geese's</u> eggs are large.

Did you notice?

In the first sentence in each pair, the underlined word shows singular ownership.
In the second, the underlined word shows plural ownership.

Do you remember?

For singular nouns, possession is shown with this mark (') + **s**.
When a plural noun ends with **s**, possession is shown by adding this mark (') after the **s**.
Some plural nouns, like **geese**, do not end with **s**.
For such plural nouns, ownership is shown by adding this mark (') + **s**.

Try it out.

For each of the following nouns, write the form that shows ownership.

1. men _____
2. calf _____
3. mice _____
4. drape _____
5. sofa _____

6. homes _____
7. babies _____
8. class _____
9. dresses _____
10. witch _____

STOP CHECK ANSWERS ON PAGE 140.

WRITING A BUSINESS LETTER

Read the following:

```
                               11 Cole Street
                               Monticello, Arkansas 71655
                               May 4, 1988

Andrew Smith
Roadway Express Company
574 First Avenue
Monticello, Arkansas 71655

Dear Mr. Smith:

   Please contact me at my office to discuss delivery of
supplies. My phone number is (501) 555-6489.

                               Sincerely yours,

                               Bob Joyce
```

Do you remember?

The heading in a business letter includes the sender's address and the date. The inside address gives the name or title and address of the person receiving the letter.

GO ON TO THE NEXT PAGE

Try it out.

This business letter is not written correctly. Write it over correctly.

```
                                21 davis boulevard
                                chicago illinois 60624
                                june 6 1990


felix garza
abc chemical company
43 second avenue
chicago illinois 60624

dear mr. garza

   the chemicals i purchased from you for my lawn ruined it.
please contact me immediately to discuss this.

                        sincerely yours,

                        greg harper
```

STOP CHECK ANSWERS ON PAGE 140.

SPELLING

Read the following:

We go to my mother's house on <u>Thanksgiving</u>.
We enjoy that <u>holiday</u>.
It is our <u>favorite</u> one.
We always have a <u>turkey</u> on Thanksgiving.
We are all <u>together</u> on Thanksgiving.

Did you know?

The underlined words in the sentences above are often misspelled.

Try it out.

Look at each word. Then cover it and write it in the blank. Check your spelling. Finally, write a sentence using the word.

1. Thanksgiving _____

_____

2. holiday _____

_____

3. favorite _____

_____

4. turkey _____

_____

5. together _____

_____

STOP CHECK SAMPLE ANSWERS ON PAGE 140.

ALPHABETIZING (USING THE DICTIONARY)

Do you remember?

A dictionary has guide words at the top of each page.
The guide words tell which are the first and last words on that page.
All words between the two guide words are on that page in alphabetical order.

Read the following:

Here is a sample of the guide words at the top of a dictionary page.

throw	timer

Try it out.

Use the guide words **throw** and **timer** to answer these questions. Write **Yes** or **No** in each blank.

1. Is the word **throat** on this page? _____

2. Is the word **tile** on this page? _____

3. Is the word **threat** on this page? _____

4. Is the word **thrill** on this page? _____

5. Is the word **through** on this page? _____

6. Is the word **think** on this page? _____

7. Is the word **three** on this page? _____

8. Is the word **thirteen** on this page? _____

9. Is the word **trail** on this page? _____

10. Is the word **tiny** on this page? _____

STOP CHECK ANSWERS ON PAGE 140.

CAPITALIZING (NAMES OF COMPANIES)
Write each of the following sentences over correctly.

1. my aunt nancy works at the abc clothing company.

_____

2. I am going west to begin work at the expert computer company.

_____

3. do you work at burger delight?

_____

4. jim haines is a salesman at george's furniture company.

_____

5. i'm a carpenter at drake construction company.

_____

AGREEMENT OF SUBJECT AND VERB
Underline the verb that is correct for each sentence.

1. John's brother (**is** or **are**) a drug user.
2. Mike's parents (**do** or **does**) not know how to help him.
3. Mike's arms (**look** or **looks**) like a pin cushion.
4. Mike's wife and children (**is** or **are**) afraid of him.
5. A drug user's relatives (**has** or **have**) a hard time.

COMBINING SENTENCES
Combine each pair in two different ways. Write two different sentences for each pair. (You may refer to the models on page 30.)

1. Many drug addicts live on my street.
   Many drug addicts sell drugs to young children.

_____

_____

GO ON TO THE NEXT PAGE

2. Parents fear for their children's lives.
   Parents don't know what to do.

   _____

   _____

3. The schools aren't safe from drugs.
   The schools have many drug dealers on their grounds.

   _____

   _____

4. Some children as young as ten are on drugs.
   Some children as young as ten do not attend school.

   _____

   _____

5. The police should do more about drugs in schools.
   The police should rid our schools of drug dealers.

   _____

   _____

THE PRONOUNS *ANYONE*, *EVERYONE*, *NO ONE*, AND *SOMEONE*

Underline the verb that is correct for the sentence.

1. Anyone (**is** or **are**) able to do that.

2. Everyone (**is** or **are**) here now.

3. Someone (**has** or **have**) it.

4. Anyone (**has** or **have**) the right to go there.

5. No one (**know** or **knows**) who he is.

PRONOUNS (SHOWING OWNERSHIP OR BELONGING TO)

Fill in each blank correctly with a pronoun that shows ownership.

1. That pet is Sara's.

   That pet is _____.

2. This is my used car.

   It is _____.

GO ON TO THE NEXT PAGE

3. These are my brother's tools.

   They are _____ .

4. Those are my parents' things.

   Those are _____ things.

5. The dog's paw is broken.

   _____ paw is broken.

REGULAR AND IRREGULAR VERBS

In the blank, write the form of each verb that shows past time.

1. bite   _____

2. try   _____

3. begin   _____

4. go   _____

5. join   _____

6. do   _____

7. stay   _____

8. drink   _____

9. work   _____

10. eat   _____

THE WORDS *WELL*, *BETTER*, AND *BEST*

Fill in each blank with a correct form of the word **well**.

1. Wing did _____ than Paolo in the race.

2. She runs the _____ of everyone.

3. Romain works _____ with others.

4. I can think _____ here than at your house.

5. Tomiko and Charlotte work and play _____ together.

SHOWING OWNERSHIP OR BELONGING TO (POSSESSION)

For each of the following nouns, write the form that shows ownership.

1. children   _____

2. James   _____

3. flower   _____

4. wages   _____

5. ladies   _____

6. mouse   _____

7. church   _____

8. box   _____

9. doctor   _____

10. wives   _____

GO ON TO THE NEXT PAGE

WRITING A BUSINESS LETTER

This business letter is not written correctly. Write it over correctly.

yours truly   dear mr jackson

benjamin helms

                    214 morris avenue
                    new york new york 10022
                    may 27, 1990

                                    walter jackson

                                    forbes clothing outlet
                                    453 center street
                                    new york new york 10003

   i ordered two pairs of work pants from you over two months
ago. i still have not received them. if i do not receive them
soon, i will cancel my order.

_____

_____

_____

_____

_____

_____

_____

_____

_____

_____

_____

GO ON TO THE NEXT PAGE

SPELLING

Use each of the following words in a sentence.

1. Thanksgiving

_____

2. holiday

_____

3. favorite

_____

4. turkey

_____

5. together

_____

ALPHABETIZING (USING THE DICTIONARY)

Use the guide words **scratch** and **scrub** to answer these questions. Write **Yes** or **No** in each blank.

1. Is the word **scream** on this page?   _____

2. Is the word **scram** on this page?   _____

3. Is the word **scrap** on this page?   _____

4. Is the word **screen** on this page?   _____

5. Is the word **scribble** on this page?   _____

STOP   CHECK ANSWERS BEGINNING ON PAGE 141.

Count how many items you answered correctly in each **Section** of the Chapter Two Review. Write your score per section in the **My Scores** column. If all of your section scores are as high as the **Good Scores**, go on to Chapter Three. If any of your section scores are lower than the **Good Scores**, study the lessons on the assigned **Review Pages** again before you go on to Chapter Three.

Section	Good Scores	My Scores	Review Pages
Capitalizing (Names of Companies)	4 or 5		26
Agreement of Subject and Verb	4 or 5		27
Combining Sentences	4 or 5		28–31
The Pronouns **Anyone**, **Everyone**, **No One**, and **Someone**	4 or 5		32
Pronouns (Showing Ownership or Belonging To)	4 or 5		33–34
Regular and Irregular Verbs	8, 9, or 10		35
The Words **Well**, **Better**, and **Best**	4 or 5		36
Showing Ownership or Belonging To (Possession)	8, 9, or 10		37
Writing a Business Letter	A correct letter		38–39
Spelling	4 or 5		40
Alphabetizing (Using the Dictionary)	4 or 5		41

CHAPTER THREE

CAPITALIZING (NAMES OF BUILDINGS)

Read the following:

Chrysler Building   Radio City Music Hall   Yankee Stadium

Did you notice?

Words in the names of buildings begin with capital letters.

Try it out.

Write each sentence over correctly.

1. i went to shea stadium to see a baseball game.

   _____

2. faye saw the empire state building when she went to new york.

   _____

3. the national bank is on center street in ohio.

   _____

4. mrs. trent sang at carnegie hall when she was younger.

   _____

5. Ed and i are going west to california to visit the coliseum.

   _____

6. my english friend visited the world trade center in february.

   _____

7. his uncle max and i went to the sears tower in chicago.

   _____

8. ben went to the drake building on foster street.

   _____

9. in may don is going south to florida to visit disney world.

   _____

10. molly was going west to seattle, washington, to see the kingdome.

    _____

STOP CHECK ANSWERS ON PAGE 142.

SINGULAR AND PLURAL SUBJECTS

Read the following:

Jim's <u>coat</u> needs cleaning.
Jim's <u>coats</u> need cleaning.

Did you notice?

The underlined word in each sentence is the noun in the complete subject
that controls the verb.
When the noun is singular, the verb is also singular.
When that noun is plural, the verb is also plural.
Nouns that show possession do not control verbs.

Try it out.

Underline the noun or nouns that control the verb in each of the following
sentences. Write **S** in the blank if the subject of the sentence is singular. Write **P**
in the blank if the subject of the sentence is plural.

1. Mei's parents are not here now. _____

2. Tomas's home is beautiful. _____

3. Their dogs need better care. _____

4. My sister's children are cute. _____

5. Yuriko's son and daughter go to school. _____

6. David's wife is having a baby. _____

7. My child's friends were hurt. _____

8. His sick aunt needs care. _____

9. The shirt's sleeve is torn. _____

10. Mrs. Duval's supper is always good. _____

STOP CHECK ANSWERS ON PAGE 142.

COMBINING SENTENCES

Read the following:
The church bell rang.
The train whistle blew.

Now read the following:
The church bell rang, and the train whistle blew.

Did you notice?
The subjects and predicates of the short sentences are different.
The two short sentences are combined in the long sentence.
A comma (,) and the word **and** are used to combine the sentences.
The combination does not shorten the sentences.

Try it out.

Write one sentence that combines the two in each of the following pairs. Follow the model above.

1. The young bride left home one night.
   Her husband never saw her again.

   _____

2. She went for a walk late at night.
   Her husband stayed behind.

   _____

3. People searched everywhere for her.
   The police questioned everyone.

   _____

4. Everyone feared the worst.
   Sometime later her body was found.

   _____

5. The young bride had been murdered.
   The police suspected the husband.

   _____

STOP CHECK ANSWERS ON PAGE 142.

COMBINING SENTENCES

Read the following:

The phone rang.
Everyone jumped to answer it.

Now read the following:

The phone rang, <u>and</u> everyone jumped to answer it.

Did you notice?

The subjects and predicates of the two sentences are different.
The two short sentences are combined in the long sentence.
A comma (,) and the word **and** are used to combine the sentences.
The combination does not shorten the sentences.

Try it out.

Write one sentence that combines the two in each of the following pairs. Follow the model above.

1. Today's single people have many concerns.
   One of them is fear of AIDS.

   _____

2. Some famous people died of AIDS.
   That helped give the disease national attention.

   _____

3. AIDS has spread widely.
   Casual sex can be dangerous.

   _____

4. Young people need to know about AIDS.
   Schools have begun to teach them.

   _____

5. Many young women today want good, strong relationships.
   Many young men desire the same.

   _____

STOP CHECK ANSWERS ON PAGE 142.

COMBINING SENTENCES

Read the following:

Sharon's job is very interesting.
Sharon's job requires a lot of energy.

Now read the following:

Sharon's job is very interesting, and it requires a lot of energy.
Sharon's job is very interesting and requires a lot of energy.

Did you notice?

The two short sentences about Sharon's job are combined in two different ways.

The first way uses a comma (,) and the words **and** and **it** in the longer sentence.

The second way uses only the word **and**. The words **Sharon's job** are written only once.

Try it out.

Combine each pair in two different ways following the models above. Write two different sentences for each pair.

1. Jeff's dog is lost.
   Jeff's dog has been missing for two days.

   _____

   _____

2. Jeff's neighbors are looking for the dog.
   Jeff's neighbors are searching everywhere.

   _____

   _____

3. Betty's husband just had a heart attack.
   Betty's husband is not doing well.

   _____

   _____

GO ON TO THE NEXT PAGE

4. Daniela's uncle is retiring soon.
Daniela's uncle is moving to another state.

_____

_____

5. Nader's brother was in an accident.
Nader's brother was badly hurt.

_____

_____

STOP CHECK ANSWERS ON PAGE 142.

THE PRONOUNS *ANYBODY, EVERYBODY, NOBODY,* AND *SOMEBODY*

Read the following:

Anybody is able to do that.
Everybody has a right to do that.
Nobody has enough money for the tickets.
Somebody needs me.

Did you notice?

The underlined words in the sentences above are pronouns.
They can stand for any person.
The words **anybody**, **everybody**, **nobody**, and **somebody** are singular, just as the word **body** is singular.
They go with singular verbs, such as **is**, **has**, and **needs**.

Try it out.

Underline the verb that is correct for the sentence.

1. Everybody (**is** or **are**) coming to my party.

2. Nobody (**need** or **needs**) to stay here with me.

3. Anybody (**has** or **have**) the power to do that.

4. Somebody (**talk** or **talks**) too much.

5. Everybody (**play** or **plays**) there.

6. Everybody (**stay** or **stays**) at my house.

7. Somebody (**has** or **have**) a cold.

8. Everybody (**know** or **knows**) us.

9. Anybody (**is** or **are**) welcome.

10. Nobody (**want** or **wants**) to help him.

STOP CHECK ANSWERS ON PAGE 142.

THE VERBS *CATCH, CATCHES, CAUGHT,* AND *WILL CATCH*

Read the following:

Libby catches the ball.   Libby and Ted catch the ball.
I caught the ball.   We caught the ball.
He will catch the ball.   They will catch the ball.

Did you notice?

The verbs **catch** and **catches** describe action in the present.
Catch goes with plural nouns and the pronouns **I, you, we,** and **they.**
Catches goes with singular nouns and the pronouns **he, she,** and **it.**
The word **caught** describes action in the past.
The words **will catch** describe action in the future.

Try it out.

Fill in each blank with **catch, catches, caught,** or **will catch.**

1. I _____ a fly ball yesterday.

2. Rita _____ a cold if she does that.

3. My dog _____ tennis balls all the time.

4. Dorothy and John _____ an early train yesterday.

5. We _____ many fish tomorrow.

6. Jerry always _____ his sister's colds.

7. Ben _____ the man before he fell off the track.

8. They _____ the 7:00 A.M. train every morning.

9. Terry _____ the same bus every night.

10. I _____ the bride's flowers at the wedding.

STOP   CHECK ANSWERS ON PAGE 142.

USING THE WORDS *HAS* AND *HAVE* WITH VERBS

Read the following:

These sentences describe actions that began and ended in the past.

Fred <u>worked</u> hard yesterday.

She <u>played</u> tennis earlier.

Fred and Dave <u>helped</u> us just before.

They <u>visited</u> us last week.

Now read the following:

These sentences describe actions that started in the past and continue to the present time.

John <u>has worked</u> hard for years.

He <u>has played</u> tennis for three years.

Sal and Irv <u>have helped</u> us every day.

They <u>have visited</u> us frequently.

Did you notice?

The words **has** and **have** are sometimes used with other verbs.

A **verb phrase** like **has worked** or **have helped** describes an action that started in the past and continues to the present time.

Try it out.

Fill in each blank with the correct verb or verb phrase.

1. Patrick and Monique _____ a number of businesses since they were married. (**started** or **have started**)

2. We _____ to do that yesterday. (**tried** or **have tried**)

3. Our new neighbors _____ in last week. (**have moved** or **moved**)

4. My friends _____ for months for an apartment and still have not found one. (**looked** or **have looked**)

5. I _____ my friend to the hospital this evening.

   (**rushed** or **have rushed**)

6. My girlfriend _____ delicious bread for me yesterday.

   (**baked** or **has baked**)

GO ON TO THE NEXT PAGE

7. Sean and Sandy _____ to Maine last summer.

   (**traveled** or **have traveled**)

8. My uncle _____ football since I was young.

   (**played** or **has played**)

9. Sonia and I _____ together for many years.

   (**worked** or **have worked**)

10. The boy _____, but he is all right now. (**has tripped** or **tripped**)

STOP   CHECK ANSWERS ON PAGE 143.

USING THE WORDS *HAS* AND *HAVE* WITH VERBS

Read the following:

These sentences describe actions that began and ended in the past.

They <u>stayed</u> too long yesterday.

Betty <u>cared</u> for her last week.

I <u>saw</u> her do that before.

We <u>thought</u> about you earlier.

Now read the following:

These sentences describe actions that started in the past and continue to the present time.

They <u>have stayed</u> too long again.

Betty <u>has cared</u> for her for many years.

I <u>have seen</u> her do that a number of times.

We <u>have thought</u> about you often.

Did you notice?

The words **has** and **have** are sometimes used with other verbs.

A verb phrase like **have stayed** or **has cared** describes an action that started in the past and continues to the present time.

Try it out.

Fill in each blank with the correct verb or verb phrase.

1. Ricardo and I _____ that for a few months.

   (**needed** or **have needed**)

2. They _____ for one hour already. (**ran** or **have run**)

3. They Rizzolis _____ their home a week ago. (**sold** or **have sold**)

4. We _____ her our new apartment. (**showed** or **have showed**)

5. King and Masami _____ many fish yesterday.

   (**caught** or **have caught**)

6. Michiko and Dominique _____ golf earlier.

   (**played** or **have played**)

GO ON TO THE NEXT PAGE

7. José and Maria _____ us to a party. (**invited** or **have invited**)

8. Hugo and Eva _____ Thanksgiving with us every year.

(**spent** or **have spent**)

9. Mrs. Sato _____ us to visit her for a long time.

(**wanted** or **has wanted**)

10. My brother _____ a lot of money last week.

(**earned** or **has earned**)

STOP CHECK ANSWERS ON PAGE 143.

ADDING *ING* TO VERBS WITH A HELPING VERB

Read the following:
The following sentences describe action that is going on right now.
   I am <u>catching</u> a cold.
   She <u>is making</u> a cake.
   We <u>are trying</u> to be cheerful.

Did you notice?
Action that is going on right now is described in a verb phrase.
The verb in the phrase ends with **ing**.
One of these helping verbs goes before the verb: **am**, **is**, or **are**.

Try it out.
In each blank, write the verb phrase that describes action that is going on right now.

1. Everyone _____ about that accident. (**talk**)

2. She _____ to buy a summer home. (**try**)

3. Jason _____ the grass. (**mow**)

4. My pets _____ their food. (**eat**)

5. Laura and Bob _____ in Maine. (**travel**)

6. He _____ some new clothes. (**buy**)

7. I _____ too much weight. (**gain**)

8. My friends _____ a party. (**plan**)

9. Fred _____ very tall. (**grow**)

10. Who _____ so soon? (**leave**)

STOP CHECK ANSWERS ON PAGE 143.

THE VERB *BE*

Try it out.

Fill in each blank with one of the forms of the verb **be** from the list above.

1. Who _____ there tomorrow?

2. We _____ at a great party last night.

3. I _____ careful about what I eat now.

4. They _____ silly earlier.

5. Héctor and César _____ friends for a long time.

6. This problem _____ going on for too long now.

7. They _____ to the beach a few times already.

8. My aunt Benita _____ a great help to us yesterday.

9. She _____ at our picnic later.

10. This year _____ a good one so far.

STOP CHECK ANSWERS ON PAGE 143.

63

CONTRACTIONS

Try it out.

There are two contractions in each of these sentences. Each of the contractions stands for two words. Write those two words in the blanks below the sentences.

1. I've had two colds so far, so I'm rather run down.

   _____   _____

2. She's going to the game, but it'll rain soon.

   _____   _____

3. They're not here yet, but they'll arrive in a minute.

   _____   _____

4. I'll stay here if you'll stay with me.

   _____   _____

5. They've eaten, but I've had nothing to eat.

   _____   _____

STOP CHECK ANSWERS ON PAGE 143.

SPELLING

Try it out.

Look at each word. Then cover it and write it in the blank. Check your spelling. Finally, write a sentence using the word.

1. enough   _____

_____

2. beginning   _____

_____

3. heard   _____

_____

4. later   _____

_____

5. sentence   _____

_____

STOP   CHECK SAMPLE ANSWERS ON PAGE 143.

ALPHABETIZING (USING THE PHONE BOOK)

Do you remember?

A phone book has guide names at the top of each page.
The guide names are people's family names.
They tell which are the first and last names on that page.
All the names between the two guide names are on that page in alphabetical order.

Now read the following:

Here is a sample of the guide names at the top of a phone book page.

Fulmer—Gallo

Did you notice?

The family name **Fulmer** is the first name on the page.
The family name **Gallo** is the last name on the page.

Try it out.

Use the guide names **Fulmer** and **Gallo** to answer the following questions. Write **Yes** or **No** in each blank.

1. Is the name **Marie Fuler** on this page? _____

2. Is the name **James Fong** on this page? _____

3. Is the name **Sara Furth** on this page? _____

4. Is the name **Mary Gage** on this page? _____

5. Is the name **Ann Gaines** on this page? _____

6. Is the name **Robert Gate** on this page? _____

7. Is the name **Nora Garcia** on this page? _____

8. Is the name **Peter Galli** on this page? _____

9. Is the name **Fred Fullino** on this page? _____

10. Is the name **Alma Fuentes** on this page? _____

STOP CHECK ANSWERS ON PAGE 143.

CAPITALIZING (NAMES OF BUILDINGS)

Write each of the following sentences over correctly.

1. aunt diane and uncle elton go to the metrodome in minneapolis to watch football games.

   _____

2. mr. carter, my father, and i go to yankee stadium to watch baseball games.

   _____

3. have you ever been to the astrodome in houston, texas?

   _____

4. no, i've only been to the superdome in new orleans, louisiana.

   _____

5. the kennedy center for performing arts is in washington, d.c.

   _____

SINGULAR AND PLURAL SUBJECTS

Underline the noun that controls the verb in each of the following sentences. Write **S** in the blank if the subject of the sentence is singular. Write **P** in the blank if the subject of the sentence is plural.

1. Mr. Carter's parents are visiting him today.   _____

2. John's wife is an excellent cook.   _____

3. My parents' apartment is rather small.   _____

4. My brothers' children are sometimes quite rude.   _____

5. That dog's bark is frightening.   _____

COMBINING SENTENCES

Write one sentence that combines the two in each of the following pairs.

1. The snowstorm is over.
   The damage has to be repaired.

   _____

GO ON TO THE NEXT PAGE

2. Bob just got a promotion.
His girlfriend found a good job.

_____

3. I lost my watch yesterday.
My wife lost hers today.

_____

4. The tickets to the show will cost a lot.
We will still not have good seats.

_____

5. I don't like meat.
My boyfriend doesn't like vegetables.

_____

COMBINING SENTENCES

Combine each pair of sentences in two different ways. Write two different sentences for each pair.

1. Sam's work is very important.
Sam's work requires long hours at the job.

_____

_____

2. John could stay longer.
John could eat dinner with us.

_____

_____

3. Tuesday was a stormy day.
Tuesday was not a good day to go out.

_____

_____

4. Sherry is an excellent supervisor.
Sherry has a group of loyal employees.

_____

_____

GO ON TO THE NEXT PAGE

5. Mr. Veldez is traveling alone.
Mr. Veldez has no baggage.

_____

_____

THE PRONOUNS *ANYBODY*, *EVERYBODY*, *NOBODY*, AND *SOMEBODY*
Underline the verb that is correct for the sentence.

1. Somebody (**is** or **are**) to blame for this.

2. Nobody (**has** or **have**) the right to go there.

3. Anybody (**is** or **are**) welcome to this.

4. Somebody (**like** or **likes**) her.

5. Everybody (**know** or **knows**) me.

THE VERBS *CATCH*, *CATCHES*, *CAUGHT*, AND *WILL CATCH*
Fill in each blank with **catch**, **catches**, **caught**, or **will catch**.

1. George _____ an early train tomorrow.

2. My father _____ every ball you throw to him.

3. He _____ a bad cold last week.

4. _____ this.

5. She _____ her heel in something before.

USING THE WORDS *HAS* AND *HAVE* WITH VERBS
Fill in each blank with the correct verb or verb phrase.

1. They _____ the same thing for years. (**tried** or **have tried**)

2. The Lees _____ a while ago to go on vacation. (**left** or **have left**)

3. I _____ to Washington every summer since I was six.

   (**traveled** or **have traveled**)

4. Sara _____ at this company for ten years.

   (**worked** or **has worked**)

5. My brother _____ in a different band last night.

   (**played** or **has played**)

GO ON TO THE NEXT PAGE

ADDING *ING* TO VERBS WITH A HELPING VERB

In each blank, write the verb phrase that describes action that is going on right now.

1. My girlfriend _____ to school here. (**go**)

2. I _____ sorry for myself. (**feel**)

3. Her old boyfriend _____ to get her back. (**try**)

4. Her friends _____ him away from her. (**keep**)

5. They _____ me. (**support**)

THE VERB *BE*

Fill in each blank with **am**, **are**, **is**, **was**, **were**, **will be**, **am being**, **are being**, **is being**, **has been**, or **have been**.

1. I _____ there later.

2. They _____ late five times already.

3. Diane _____ out of work for the past month.

4. They _____ difficult, as usual.

5. The twins _____ at our house earlier today.

CONTRACTIONS

There are two contractions in each of these sentences. Each of the contractions stands for two words. Write those two words in the blanks below the sentences.

1. I'll see you later after I've had some rest.

   _____   _____

2. They'll stay too long, so we'll have to leave without them.

   _____   _____

3. He's very nice, but he's having some problems.

   _____   _____

4. We've planned too many things to do, but we'll do them.

   _____   _____

5. It's been beautiful for two days now, but it's going to rain later.

   _____   _____

GO ON TO THE NEXT PAGE

SPELLING

Use each of the following words in a sentence.

1. enough

   _____

2. beginning

   _____

3. heard

   _____

4. later

   _____

5. sentence

   _____

ALPHABETIZING (USING THE PHONE BOOK)

Use the guide names **Carter** and **Carver** to answer the following questions.
Write **Yes** or **No** in each blank.

1. Is the name **Enya Carrido** on this page?   _____

2. Is the name **Pablo Cárdenas** on this page?   _____

3. Is the name **Laurent Cartier** on this page? _____

4. Is the name **Julio Carzo** on this page?   _____

5. Is the name **Saúl Carvajal** on this page?   _____

STOP   CHECK ANSWERS BEGINNING ON PAGE 143.

Count how many items you answered correctly in each **Section** of the Chapter Three Review. Write your score per section in the **My Scores** column. If all of your section scores are as high as the **Good Scores**, go on to Chapter Four. If any of your section scores are lower than the **Good Scores**, study the lessons on the assigned **Review Pages** again before you go on to Chapter Four.

Section	Good Scores	My Scores	Review Pages
Capitalizing (Names of Buildings)	4 or 5		50
Singular and Plural Subjects	4 or 5		51
Combining Sentences	4 or 5		52–53
Combining Sentences	4 or 5		54–55
The Pronouns **Anybody**, **Everybody**, **Nobody**, and **Somebody**	4 or 5		56
The Verbs **Catch**, **Catches**, **Caught**, and **Will Catch**	4 or 5		57
Using the Words **Has** and **Have** with Verbs	4 or 5		58–61
Adding **ing** to Verbs with a Helping Verb	4 or 5		62
The Verb **Be**	4 or 5		63
Contractions	4 or 5		64
Spelling	4 or 5		65
Alphabetizing (Using the Phone Book)	4 or 5		66

CHAPTER FOUR

CAPITALIZING (COMMON NOUNS AND PROPER NOUNS)

Read the following:

COMMON NOUNS	PROPER NOUNS
city	San Francisco
state	New York
avenue	Second Avenue
war	World War II
man	Mr. Veldez
woman	Mrs. Tong
person	Aunt Jane
language	Spanish

Do you remember?

A common noun names a type of person or thing.
Common nouns are not capitalized.
A proper noun names a specific person or thing.
Proper nouns are capitalized.

Try it out.

Correct the following nouns that are capitalized incorrectly. Put a **C** in the blank by those that are correct.

1. uncle ramon _____
2. french _____
3. korean war _____
4. month _____
5. Winter _____
6. february _____
7. east berlin _____
8. miami _____
9. valentine's day _____
10. john l. sullivan _____

11. Onion _____
12. Cousin _____
13. rat _____
14. puerto rico _____
15. Star _____
16. evening _____
17. Fall _____
18. Summer _____
19. ms. tsu _____
20. Crow _____

STOP CHECK ANSWERS ON PAGE 144.

74

COMBINING SENTENCES

Try it out.
Write one sentence that combines the two in each of the following pairs. Follow
the model above.

1. My husband invited his friend to dinner.
   I do not have enough food in the house.

   _____

   _____

2. My husband should ask me first.
   He never does.

   _____

3. It makes me very angry.
   My husband doesn't seem to care.

   _____

4. Now I have to run to the store.
   I do not have enough time.

   _____

5. I could try to phone my husband.
   He probably left work already.

   _____

STOP CHECK ANSWERS ON PAGE 144.

COMBINING SENTENCES

Read the following:
My brother wants to be on the basketball team.
He is too short.

His friend, Hector, is rather tall.
He is perfect for the team.

Now read the following:
My brother wants to be on the basketball team, but he is too short.
His friend, Hector, is rather tall, and he is perfect for the team.

Did you notice?
The short sentences about my brother are combined with a comma (,) and the word **but**.
There is a contrast between the ideas in those two sentences.
The sentences about his friend are combined with a comma (,) and the word **and**.
The ideas in those two sentences support each other.

Try it out.
Write one sentence that combines the two in each of the following pairs. Use a comma with **and** or **but** in the sentence you write.

1. I hate staying home on a Saturday night.
   No one asked me to go out.

   _____

   _____

2. Some women ask men out.
   I just can't seem to do that.

   _____

   _____

3. Usually I go out with my friends.
   Tonight they are all busy.

   _____

   _____

GO ON TO THE NEXT PAGE

4. I like to go to movies by myself.
I might do that.

_____

_____

5. The night is still young.
I am going to do something exciting.

_____

_____

STOP CHECK ANSWERS ON PAGE 144.

DIRECT QUOTATIONS

Read the following:
Carol said, "She is a lovely person."
Lan said, "Yes, I agree with you."

Did you notice?
A **direct quotation** gives the exact words of a speaker.
A comma (,) goes after the word **said**.
Quotation marks (" ") go around the speaker's words.
The first word of a direct quotation is capitalized.
The period (.) at the end of the quotation is inside the quotation marks.

Try it out.
Write these direct quotations correctly.

1. He said I am happy.

   _____

2. Elias said please send this to Olga.

   _____

3. Kiyo said Hideo and I are going to visit our aunt.

   _____

4. Mrs. Matos said teaching is difficult work.

   _____

5. Martin said my son is a movie star.

   _____

6. Bijan said this year has been a hard one for me.

   _____

7. Mr. Huang said Ben's boss is firing him.

   _____

GO ON TO THE NEXT PAGE

8. Miss Moulin said things will get better soon.

_____

9. Ms. Nomura said Sally started a silly story about him.

_____

10. Bob said the new plant is very nice.

_____

STOP CHECK ANSWERS ON PAGE 145.

DIRECT AND INDIRECT QUOTATIONS

Read the following:

DIRECT QUOTATION: Ben said, "I need more time to study."

INDIRECT QUOTATION: Ben said that he needs more time to study.

Did you notice?

A **direct quotation** gives the exact words of the speaker.

An **indirect quotation** tells what the speaker said but does not use the speaker's exact words.

There is no special punctuation in an indirect quotation.

Do you remember?

A comma (,) goes after the word **said** in a direct quotation.

Quotation marks (" ") go around the speaker's words.

The first word of a direct quotation is capitalized.

The period (.) at the end of the quotation is inside the quotation marks.

Try it out.

Each of the following sentences is a quotation, direct or indirect. Write the direct quotations over correctly. Write **IQ** in any blank that follows an indirect quotation.

1. He said that he was happy.

   _____

2. He said that is not a nice thing to do.

   _____

3. Sing said that he would be here soon.

   _____

4. She said no, I am not going with you.

   _____

5. Leila said that she got the job she wanted.

   _____

6. Tony said that his job is very important to him.

   _____

GO ON TO THE NEXT PAGE

7. Henry said I want to learn more about this subject.

_____

8. Arturo said that his car ran out of gas.

_____

9. Aurora said that her mother was feeling better.

_____

10. Yasuko said Hidori does not want to meet us.

_____

STOP CHECK ANSWERS ON PAGE 145.

THE PRONOUNS *WHO*, *WHOM*, AND *WHOSE*

Read the following:

Who called me?
To whom are you giving that?
Whose coat is this?

Did you notice?

The pronouns **who**, **whom**, and **whose** can be used to ask questions.
The pronoun **who** is the subject of a sentence.
The pronoun **whom** is used after words such as **about**, **against**, **among**, **around**, **before**, **below**, **beneath**, **between**, **for**, **of**, **on**, **to**, **under**, and **with**.
The pronoun **whose** is used to show ownership.

Try it out.

Fill in each blank with **who**, **whom**, or **whose**.

1. _____ is there?

2. About _____ are you talking?

3. _____ hat is that?

4. _____ did that terrible thing?

5. With _____ are you going?

6. Against _____ are you playing?

7. _____ brother is he?

8. _____ dog is that?

9. _____ bought me this nice gift?

10. _____ house is that?

STOP CHECK ANSWERS ON PAGE 145.

USING THE WORDS *HAS* AND *HAVE* WITH VERBS

Read the following:

PRESENT	PAST	UP TO NOW
It blows.	It blew.	It has blown.
I break dates.	I broke dates.	I have broken dates.
They see well.	They saw well.	They have seen well.

Did you notice?

The verbs above are irregular.
They have special forms to describe action in the past.
They have special forms when they are used with **has** or **have**.

Do you remember?

When a verb is used with **has** or **have**, it describes action that began in the past and continues to the present time.

Try it out.

Fill in each blank with the correct verb or verb phrase.

1. He _____ me a great deal a lot the past three months.
   (**saw** or **has seen**)

2. We _____ her to be the chairperson last night.
   (**chose** or **have chosen**)

3. My little brother _____ my expensive computer yesterday.
   (**broke** or **has broken**)

4. Haruo _____ his promise three times already.
   (**broke** or **has broken**)

5. Tom _____ to me every day since he left. (**wrote** or **has written**)

6. I _____ to your house yesterday. (**came** or **have come**)

7. Gale _____ her toe earlier. (**broke** or **has broken**)

8. Miguel _____ not to go to the party last night.
   (**chose** or **has chosen**)

9. Kathy and I _____ here from Utah. (**came** or **have come**)

10. We _____ a bad movie three times in a row.
    (**chose** or **have chosen**)

STOP CHECK ANSWERS ON PAGE 145.

ADDING *ING* TO VERBS WITH A HELPING VERB

Read the following:

The man is hurrying to catch the bus.
They are singing in the show.
She is baking a chocolate cake.

Do you remember?

Action that is going on right now is described in a verb phrase.
The verb in the phrase ends with **ing**.
One of these words goes before that verb: **am**, **is**, or **are**.

Now read the following:

Some verbs, such as **bake**, end with a silent **e**.
That **e** is dropped when the **ing** ending is used.

Try it out.

In each blank, write the verb phrase that describes action that is going on right now.

1. We _____ of giving her a present. (**think**)

2. She _____ to the beach. (**drive**)

3. My mother _____ the cake for the party. (**bake**)

4. Mario and Ester _____ home at this moment. (**drive**)

5. Who _____ that light? (**shine**)

6. Akemi and I _____ into the pool. (**dive**)

7. We _____ hard. (**try**)

8. They _____ away from the fire. (**move**)

9. Kin _____ his finger nails. (**file**)

10. The dog _____ my slipper. (**bite**)

STOP   CHECK ANSWERS ON PAGE 145.

ADVERBS

Read the following:

Frank works <u>harder</u> than George.
He works the <u>hardest</u> of all.

Sally speaks <u>more softly</u> than Jane.
She speaks the <u>most softly</u> of all.

Do you remember?

Many adverbs end with **er** or **est** when they compare actions.
The word **more** or **most** goes before other adverbs when they compare actions.
Some adverbs, such as **often**, can show comparison either way.

Try it out.

In each blank, write the comparing form of the adverb correctly.

1. They spoke _____ of Mohammed than of Mehdi. (**proudly**)

2. We drive the _____ of all. (**carefully**)

3. My cat drinks the _____ of any cat. (**fast**)

4. He left _____ than Rafael. (**quietly**)

5. Marisol dresses _____ than her mother. (**beautifully**)

6. We help them the _____. (**often**)

7. The deer runs _____ than other animals. (**swiftly**)

8. The dog growled _____ than the others. (**fiercely**)

9. The girl spoke _____ today than yesterday. (**happily**)

10. That child yells _____ than mine. (**loud**)

STOP CHECK ANSWERS ON PAGE 145.

THE COMMA

Read the following:

The <u>cranky old</u> man yelled at us.
He wore an <u>ugly red</u> sweater.
He never had a <u>cute little</u> child.

The <u>cranky, loud</u> man yelled at us.
He wore an <u>ugly, wrinkled</u> sweater.
He never had a <u>cute, intelligent</u> child.

Did you notice?

Each sentence has two adjectives.
There is no comma between two adjectives when the second adjective describes age, color, or size.
There is usually a comma between two adjectives at other times.

Try it out.

Each of the following sentences has two adjectives. Add commas between adjectives where they are needed. If a sentence needs no comma, write **NC** in the blank following the sentence.

1. The little white cat ran away. _____

2. The tired old woman walked slowly. _____

3. The sad sick dog looked at us. _____

4. The good kind woman helped us. _____

5. My new green jacket is my favorite. _____

6. This is a lovely black hat. _____

7. I like my funny old hat. _____

8. The hungry tired hikers returned late. _____

9. The itchy rough sweater bothers me. _____

10. The kind hardworking woman smiled at me. _____

STOP CHECK ANSWERS ON PAGE 145.

86

THE WORDS *A* AND *AN*

Read the following:

an angel	an animal	a book	a cold	an eagle
an egg	an hour	a house	an icicle	an Indian
a mouse	a nose	a union	an unwashed child	
an x-ray	a year	a zoo		

Do you remember?

The word **a** goes before words that begin with a consonant sound.
The word **an** goes before words that begin with a vowel sound.

Try it out.

Put **a** or **an** before each of the following.

1. _____ underweight person

2. _____ eager child

3. _____ unsolved mystery

4. _____ yard

5. _____ orange

6. _____ pie

7. _____ ice cream pop

8. _____ hourglass

9. _____ park bench

10. _____ apricot

11. _____ owl

12. _____ ruler

13. _____ early bus

14. _____ farmer

15. _____ garden

16. _____ hole

17. _____ jar

18. _____ yam

19. _____ son

20. _____ elevator

STOP CHECK ANSWERS ON PAGE 145.

WRITING A BUSINESS LETTER

Do you remember?

The heading in a business letter includes the sender's address and the date.
The inside address gives the name or title and address of the person receiving the letter.
The greeting is followed by a colon (:).

Try it out.

Write a letter in which you answer an ad for a job as a file clerk. Write to **Joan Forbes, Personnel Manager, Best Paper Company**, 111 Beaver Street, Cleveland, Ohio 44101.

STOP CHECK SAMPLE LETTER ON PAGE 146.

88

SPELLING

Try it out.

Look at each word. Then cover it and write it in the blank. Check your spelling. Finally, write a sentence using the word.

1. excellent   _____

_____

2. finally   _____

_____

3. whether   _____

_____

4. niece   _____

_____

5. science   _____

_____

STOP CHECK SAMPLE ANSWERS ON PAGE 146.

ALPHABETIZING (USING THE DICTIONARY)

Do you remember?

A dictionary has guide words at the top of each page.
The guide words tell which are the first and last words on that page.
All words between the two guide words are on that page in alphabetical order.

Read the following:

Here is a sample of the guide words at the top of a dictionary page.

clock   creek

Try it out.

Use the guide words **clock** and **creek** to answer these questions. Write **Yes** or **No** in each blank.

1. Is the word **cloak** on this page? _____

2. Is the word **club** on this page? _____

3. Is the word **clue** on this page? _____

4. Is the word **clean** on this page? _____

5. Is the word **crawl** on this page? _____

6. Is the word **closet** on this page? _____

7. Is the word **clear** on this page? _____

8. Is the word **cramp** on this page? _____

9. Is the word **clothes** on this page? _____

10. Is the word **creep** on this page? _____

STOP CHECK ANSWERS ON PAGE 146.

CAPITALIZING (COMMON NOUNS AND PROPER NOUNS)

Correct the following nouns that are capitalized incorrectly. Put a **C** in the blank by those that are correct.

1. cousin _____

2. miss ann maloney _____

3. uncle Herbert _____

4. season _____

5. News _____

6. center _____

7. disneyland _____

8. Winter _____

9. bank _____

10. italian _____

COMBINING SENTENCES

Write one sentence that combines the two in each of the following pairs.

1. The doorbell rang.
   Nobody was there.

   _____

2. The doctors did not expect the boy to live.
   His parents felt there was still a chance.

   _____

   _____

3. The plane landed safely.
   The passengers were still very frightened.

   _____

   _____

4. Pablo and Marco went hunting.
   We decided to stay home.

   _____

5. Ramona and Matsue worked hard all day.
   Their friends went to the beach.

   _____

   _____

GO ON TO THE NEXT PAGE

COMBINING SENTENCES

Write one sentence that combines the two in each of the following pairs. Use a comma with **and** or **but** in the sentence you write.

1. The sky was cloudy.
   It didn't rain.

   _____

   _____

2. Jane is an excellent student.
   Her sister Mary does not do well in school.

   _____

   _____

3. My brother is dating my best girlfriend.
   My sister is dating my best friend's brother.

   _____

   _____

4. She deserves the punishment.
   I feel sorry for her.

   _____

   _____

5. Vacations are my favorite times.
   I make the most of them.

   _____

   _____

DIRECT QUOTATIONS

Write these direct quotations correctly.

1. Choi said hold this for me until later.

   _____

2. She said the movers are coming soon.

   _____

3. I said don't go there yet.

   _____

GO ON TO THE NEXT PAGE

4. He said the new owners seem to be nice people.

_____

5. Fabio said this is the last time we move.

_____

DIRECT AND INDIRECT QUOTATIONS

Each of the following sentences is a quotation, direct or indirect. Write the **direct** quotations over correctly. Write **IQ** in the blank that follows an indirect quotation.

1. Gary said that he is very happy about this new job.

_____

2. He said I can't wait to start work tomorrow.

_____

3. His girlfriend said that she was very happy for him.

_____

4. I said that I would like a job like his.

_____

5. His friend said good luck on your new job tomorrow.

_____

THE PRONOUNS *WHO, WHOM,* AND *WHOSE*

Fill in each blank with **who**, **whom**, or **whose**.

1. About _____ are you speaking?

2. To _____ did you speak about that?

3. _____ coat is that?

4. _____ is going with you?

5. _____ gloves are these?

USING THE WORDS *HAS* AND *HAVE* WITH VERBS

Fill in the blanks with the correct verb or verb phrase.

1. They _____ that about ten times already. (**did** or **have done**)

2. Donato _____ there many times already. (**went** or **has gone**)

GO ON TO THE NEXT PAGE

3. Ling _____ a good story yesterday. (**wrote** or **has written**)

4. Who _____ the ball before? (**caught** or **has caught**)

5. Enrique _____ us to his house five times. (**invited** or **has invited**)

ADDING *ING* TO VERBS WITH A HELPING VERB

In each blank, write the verb phrase that describes action that is going on right now.

1. Rodrico _____ about getting married. (**think**)

2. Angie _____ for a place of her own. (**look**)

3. Mike _____ to change his life. (**try**)

4. Franco _____ away for a short time. (**stay**)

5. Angela _____ herself on 1,000 calories a day. (**starve**)

ADVERBS

In each blank, write the comparing form of the adverb correctly.

1. Mary spoke _____ to the child than to her husband. (**kindly**)

2. These pants ripped _____ than my other pair. (**quickly**)

3. My friend drives _____ than my brother. (**carefully**)

4. Sharon speaks the _____ of her husband. (**proudly**)

5. They work the _____ of everybody. (**slow**)

THE COMMA

Each of the following sentences has two adjectives. Add commas between adjectives where they are needed. If a sentence needs no comma, write **NC** in the blank.

1. The cute little child waved at us.   _____

2. The dirty angry animal growled at us.   _____

3. My faithful old dog is not feeling well. _____

4. Her cheerful beautiful sister is here.   _____

5. This is a nice homey place.   _____

GO ON TO THE NEXT PAGE

THE WORDS *A* AND *AN*

Put **a** or **an** before each of the following.

1. _____ ash tray

2. _____ airline pilot

3. _____ homely person

4. _____ handsome man

5. _____ ill child

6. _____ open window

7. _____ color

8. _____ gorgeous woman

9. _____ unusual day

10. _____ errand

WRITING A BUSINESS LETTER

Write a letter in which you answer an ad for a cashier position in a supermarket. Address your letter to **Michael Mahoney, Manager, Great Food Stores, 121 Main Street**, Chicago, Illinois 60653.

GO ON TO THE NEXT PAGE

SPELLING

Use each of the following words in a sentence.

1. excellent

_____

2. finally

_____

3. whether

_____

4. niece

_____

5. science

_____

ALPHABETIZING (USING THE DICTIONARY)

Use the guide words **wages** and **want** to answer the questions. Write **Yes** or **No** in each blank.

1. Is the word **waste** on this page? _____

2. Is the word **wallet** on this page? _____

3. Is the word **wave** on this page? _____

4. Is the word **water** on this page? _____

5. Is the word **wade** on this page? _____

STOP CHECK ANSWERS BEGINNING ON PAGE 146.

Count how many items you answered correctly in each **Section** of the Chapter Five Review. Write your score per section in the **My Scores** column. If all of your section scores are as high as the **Good Scores**, go on to Chapter Five. If any of your section scores are lower than the **Good Scores**, study the lessons on the assigned **Review Pages** again before you go on to Chapter Five.

Section	Good Scores	My Scores	Review Pages
Capitalizing (Common Nouns and Proper Nouns)	8, 9, or 10		74
Combining Sentences	4 or 5		75
Combining Sentences	4 or 5		76–77
Direct Quotations	4 or 5		78–79
Direct and Indirect Quotations	4 or 5		80–81
The Pronouns **Who**, **Whom**, and **Whose**	4 or 5		82
Using the Words **Has** and **Have** with Verbs	4 or 5		83
Adding **ing** to Verbs with a Helping Verb	4 or 5		84
Adverbs	4 or 5		85
The Comma	4 or 5		86
The Words **A** and **An**	8, 9, or 10		87
Writing a Business Letter	A correct letter		88
Spelling	4 or 5		89
Alphabetizing (Using the Dictionary)	4 or 5		90

CHAPTER FIVE

CAPITALIZING (COMMON NOUNS AND PROPER NOUNS)

Read the following:

COMMON NOUNS	PROPER NOUNS
title	Mrs. Rubio
month	February
person	Uncle Koyi
business	ABC Electrical Company
bank	Citibank
country	Argentina
building	Chrysler Building
movie	The Color Purple

Do you remember?

A common noun names a type of person or thing.
Common nouns are not capitalized.
A proper noun names a specific person or thing.
Proper nouns are capitalized.

Try it out.

Correct the following nouns that are capitalized incorrectly. Put a **C** in the blank by those that are correct.

1. xyz company _____
2. italy _____
3. Civil War _____
4. voter _____
5. summer _____
6. Ms. veldez _____
7. Hospital _____
8. Tokyo _____
9. halloween _____
10. mother maria _____

11. sister _____
12. spelling _____
13. Tennis _____
14. north America _____
15. stone _____
16. bank _____
17. game _____
18. english _____
19. mercy hospital _____
20. general _____

STOP CHECK ANSWERS ON PAGE 147.

COMBINING SENTENCES

Try it out.

Write one sentence that combines the two in each of the following pairs. Follow the model above.

1. I enjoy going out.
   My husband likes to stay home.

   _____

2. My husband likes to watch football games on TV.
   I hate watching sports.

   _____

3. I am an excellent dancer.
   My husband doesn't dance well at all.

   _____

4. I want to have a large family.
   My husband doesn't want any children.

   _____

5. My husband is a nice person.
   We have a lot of problems.

   _____

STOP CHECK ANSWERS ON PAGE 147.

COMBINING SENTENCES

Read the following:
Dress quickly.
We will be very late.

Now read the following:
Dress quickly, or we will be very late.

Did you notice?
The subjects and predicates of the short sentences are different.
The two short sentences are combined in the long sentence.
A comma (,) and the word **or** are used to combine the sentences.
Or is used because the ideas in the short sentences are choices.

Try it out.
Write one sentence that combines the two in each of the following pairs. Follow the model above.

1. My husband and I have to settle our differences.
   I will leave him.

   _____

2. He will talk with me about our problems.
   We will have to see a marriage counselor.

   _____

3. He has to do something.
   I will divorce him.

   _____

4. He will have to change.
   I will leave him.

   _____

5. He will make some changes.
   I will make some changes for him.

   _____

STOP CHECK ANSWERS ON PAGE 147.

COMBINING SENTENCES

Read the following:

Take care of your cut.
It will become infected.

I treated it.
It became infected anyway.

I made an appointment.
The doctor took care of the cut.

Now read the following:

Take care of your cut, or it will become infected.
I treated it, but it became infected anyway.
I made an appointment, and the doctor took care of the cut.

Did you notice?

Each pair of short sentences is combined with a comma (,) and the word **or**, **but**, or **and**. The use of **or**, **but**, or **and** depends on sentence meaning.

Try it out.

Write one sentence that combines the two in each of the following pairs. Use a comma with **or**, **but**, or **and** in the sentence you write.

1. Life has its downs.
   It also has its ups.

   _____

2. I have to work very hard.
   My family would not have very much.

   _____

3. My wife helps us a lot.
   Our children work after school.

   _____

4. Together we do well.
   It is very hard.

   _____

5. One day our ship will come in.
   I don't think it will come very soon.

   _____

STOP CHECK ANSWERS ON PAGE 147.

DIRECT QUOTATIONS

Read the following:

Federico asked, "Who is visiting us tomorrow?"
Elvira asked, "What should I wear?"

Did you notice?

A direct quotation gives the exact words of a speaker.
The quotation can be a question.
A comma goes after the word **asked**.
Quotation marks (" ") go around the speaker's words.
The first word of a direct quotation is capitalized.
The question mark (**?**) at the end of the quotation is inside the quotation marks.

Try it out.

Write these direct quotations correctly.

1. Yukio asked why are you going there?

   _____

2. Trevor asked which way should we go?

   _____

3. Betty asked how old is she?

   _____

4. Nicholas asked what is the name of our new boss?

   _____

5. Carol asked how much did you pay for that?

   _____

6. Marta asked what is the best way to do this?

   _____

7. Henry asked who made her cry?

   _____

GO ON TO THE NEXT PAGE

8. George asked why can't I go there tomorrow?

_____

9. Barbara asked which person is going to jail?

_____

10. Ken asked how can we finish that by tomorrow?

_____

STOP CHECK ANSWERS ON PAGE 148.

DIRECT AND INDIRECT QUOTATIONS

Read the following:

These sentences contain direct quotations.

Angel said, "I need more time."

Christine said, "I want to buy a new dress."

These sentences contain indirect quotations.

Angel said that he needs more time.

Christine said that she wants to buy a new dress.

Did you notice?

A direct quotation can be changed to an indirect quotation.

Do you remember?

A direct quotation gives the exact words of the speaker.

An indirect quotation tells what the speaker said, but does not use the speaker's words.

There is no special punctuation in an indirect quotation.

Try it out.

The following sentences contain direct quotations. Write each sentence over so that it contains an indirect quotation.

1. She said, "I do not want to stay here."

   _____

2. He said, "Jaime was promoted yesterday."

   _____

3. Joseph said, "We need to know more about that."

   _____

4. Benito said, "Jane is going to visit her sister today."

   _____

5. Paul said, "My best friend is getting married tomorrow."

   _____

STOP CHECK ANSWERS ON PAGE 148.

END MARKS (PUNCTUATION)

Read the following:

He asked who that person was.
Who is that person?

Did you notice?

The first sentence does not ask a question.
Because it makes a statement, it ends with a period.
The second sentence asks a question.
It ends with a question mark.

Try it out.

Put the correct end mark at the end of each sentence.

1. Sharon asked why he didn't go to the store

2. My brother asked where to meet us

3. Kimiko asked what we were going to wear later

4. Does she say that she can come with us

5. What did she want

6. Dara asked why we weren't ready yet

7. Monique asked what was happening at work

8. Is she still going with your brother

9. She asked if she could help us

10. Does Juan care much for his family

STOP CHECK ANSWERS ON PAGE 148.

THE PRONOUNS *WHO, WHOM,* AND *WHOSE*

Read the following:

Who is here?
For whom are you working?
Whose girlfriend is she?

Did you notice?

The pronouns **who**, **whom**, and **whose** can be used to ask questions.
The pronoun **who** is the subject of a sentence.
The pronoun **whom** is used after words such as **about**, **against**, **among**, **around**, **before**, **below**, **beneath**, **between**, **for**, **of**, **on**, **to**, **under**, and **with**.
The pronoun **whose** is used to show ownership.

Try it out.

Fill in each blank with **who**, **whom**, or **whose**.

1. _____ house is that?

2. With _____ did you study?

3. _____ is the new boss?

4. To _____ are you going later?

5. _____ cup are you getting?

6. On _____ did you put the blame?

7. _____ brought the dog to work?

8. _____ has seen Dolores?

9. _____ birthday is it?

10. _____ needs some help?

STOP CHECK ANSWERS ON PAGE 148.

USING THE WORDS *HAS* AND *HAVE* WITH VERBS

Read the following:

PRESENT	PAST	UP TO NOW
It begins.	It began.	It has begun.
I bite.	I bit.	I have bitten.
They drink.	They drank.	They have drunk.
We eat.	We ate.	We have eaten.
You get it.	You got it.	You have gotten it.
She goes.	She went.	She has gone.
It grows.	It grew.	It has grown.
I know.	I knew.	I have known.
He runs.	He ran.	He has run.
We take it.	We took it.	We have taken it.

Do you remember?

Irregular verbs have special forms for the past and for the time up to now. When a verb is used in a verb phrase with **has** or **have**, it describes action that began in the past and continues to the present time.

Try it out.

Fill in each blank with the correct verb or verb phrase.

1. They _____ away last night. (**have gone** or **went**)

2. Berto and I _____ in the race very year. (**have run** or **ran**)

3. Miss Oguri _____ her heel in a hole just before.

   (**has caught** or **caught**)

4. I _____ six glasses of milk yesterday. (**have drunk** or **drank**)

5. We _____ our money's worth up to now. (**have gotten** or **got**)

6. Marjan _____ him for a long time. (**has known** or **knew**)

7. Huang _____ carrots every year. (**has grown** or **grew**)

8. Luz _____ us out to dinner. (**has taken** or **took**)

9. We _____ classes last week. (**have begun** or **began**)

10. The children _____ to their mother. (**have run** or **ran**)

STOP CHECK ANSWERS ON PAGE 148.

ADDING *ING* TO VERBS WITH A HELPING VERB

Read the following:

I <u>am biking</u> to the store.
Mary <u>is walking</u> to the movies.
They <u>are playing</u> a game.
Dick and Jane <u>are working</u> hard.

Do you remember?

Action that is going on right now is described in a verb phrase.
The verb in the phrase ends with **ing**.
One of these words goes before that verb: **am**, **is**, or **are**.
The silent **e** at the end of verbs like **bike** is dropped when the **ing** ending is used.

Try it out.

In each blank, write the verb phrase that describes action that is going on right now.

1. Yoshiko _____ a book about her life. (**write**)

2. Gustavo and Gloria _____ a new house. (**build**)

3. We _____ for them here. (**wait**)

4. They _____ here now. (**stay**)

5. Sang _____ well in his new job. (**do**)

6. Irene _____ to work on time now. (**go**)

7. Olivier _____ very tall. (**grow**)

8. Susan and Henry _____ lies again. (**tell**)

9. The little baby _____. (**cry**)

10. The clothes _____ nicely. (**dry**)

STOP   CHECK ANSWERS ON PAGE 148.

THE VERB *BE*

Read the following:

Bob <u>was</u> sad about leaving his job.

They <u>were</u> here yesterday.

Mr. Smith <u>has been</u> the head of this company for years.

They <u>have been</u> here for hours.

Do you remember?

There are several forms of the verb **be**.

These are some of the forms:

TIME	FORM OF **BE**
Past	was, were
From Before to Now	has been, have been

Try it out.

Fill in each blank with one of the forms of **be** from the list above.

1. We _____ here for five hours already.

2. They _____ with us for a long time.

3. The workers _____ not happy about the strike.

4. I _____ upset yesterday.

5. My cat _____ acting strange for days.

6. Henry and I _____ tired after our long walk.

7. It _____ very dark at the beach last night.

8. Her sister _____ a nurse in the war.

9. He _____ a police officer for ten years.

10. She _____ the boss here for five years.

STOP CHECK ANSWERS ON PAGE 148.

Read the following:

Mike always <u>forgets</u>.   Mike and Fred always <u>forget</u>.
She <u>forgot</u> to do it.   They <u>forgot</u> to do it.
I <u>will forget</u>.   We <u>will forget</u>.
She <u>has forgotten</u>.   They <u>have forgotten</u>.
He <u>had forgotten</u>.   They <u>had forgotten</u>.

Did you notice?

The verbs **forgets** and **forget** describe action in the present.
Forget goes with plural nouns and the pronouns **I**, **you**, **we**, and **they**.
Forgets goes with singular nouns and the pronouns **he**, **she**, and **it**.
The word **forgot** describes action in the past.
The words **will forget** describe action in the future.
Forgotten goes with the helping verbs **has**, **have**, and **had**.

Try it out.

Fill in each blank with **forget**, **forgets**, **forgot**, **will forget**, or **forgotten**.

1. César _____ to take his medicine this morning.

2. We _____ the whole matter tomorrow.

3. I had _____ all about that.

4. The twins _____ to go earlier.

5. They have _____ them by now.

6. James _____ his girlfriend's birthday yesterday.

7. The plumbers had _____ about the leak.

8. She has _____ about that sad story.

9. David and I _____ many things now.

10. Nora _____ to meet us later.

STOP CHECK ANSWERS ON PAGE 148.

SPELLING

Read the following:

I love to eat <u>vegetables</u>.
We have a good <u>marriage</u>.
I have <u>written</u> to her already.
We are meeting on <u>Thursday</u>.
He is <u>sincerely</u> sorry.

Did you know?
The underlined words in the sentences above are often misspelled.

Try it out.

Look at each word. Then cover it and write it in the blank. Check your spelling.
Finally, write a sentence using the word.

1. vegetables _____

_____

2. marriage _____

_____

3. written _____

_____

4. Thursday _____

_____

5. sincerely _____

_____

STOP CHECK SAMPLE ANSWERS ON PAGE 148.

ALPHABETIZING (USING THE DICTIONARY)

Do you remember?

A dictionary has guide words at the top of each page.
The guide words tell which are the first and last words on that page.
All words between the two guide words are on that page in alphabetical order.

Read the following:

Here is a sample of the guide words at the top of a dictionary page.

scratch	search

Try it out.

Use the guide words **scratch** and **search** to answer these questions. Write **Yes** or **No** in each blank.

1. Is the word **scramble** on this page? _____

2. Is the word **screech** on this page? _____

3. Is the word **screen** on this page? _____

4. Is the word **scarf** on this page? _____

5. Is the word **scream** on this page? _____

6. Is the word **seek** on this page? _____

7. Is the word **seal** on this page? _____

8. Is the word **scrub** on this page? _____

9. Is the word **scribble** on this page? _____

10. Is the word **season** on this page? _____

STOP CHECK ANSWERS ON PAGE 148.

CAPITALIZING (COMMON NOUNS AND PROPER NOUNS)

Correct the following nouns that are capitalized incorrectly. Put a **C** in the blank by those that are correct.

1. brother _____
2. mexico _____
3. aunt kim _____
4. march _____
5. soldier _____

6. carnegie center _____
7. prison _____
8. chinese _____
9. building _____
10. general _____

COMBINING SENTENCES

Write one sentence that combines the two in each of the following pairs.

1. The show was funny.
   We didn't like it.

   _____

2. I enjoy watching television.
   The commercials bother me.

   _____

3. My fiancé is not very popular.
   I like him, anyway.

   _____

4. Fred's husband saw the attacker.
   His wife didn't want him to go to the police.

   _____

   _____

5. Many persons saw the attacker.
   They did nothing about him.

   _____

   _____

GO ON TO THE NEXT PAGE

COMBINING SENTENCES

Write one sentence that combines the two in each of the following pairs.

1. Do it now.
   We will have difficulty later on.

   _____

2. She will continue to go to school.
   Her parents will not support her.

   _____

3. You have to work harder.
   Your boss will probably fire you.

   _____

4. Eat your vegetables now.
   I will not give you any dessert.

   _____

5. Frank needs to exercise more.
   He will get much fatter.

   _____

COMBINING SENTENCES

Write one sentence that combines the two in each of the following pairs. Use a comma with **or**, **but**, or **and** in the sentence you write.

1. That was the hardest thing to do.
   I had to do it.

   _____

2. No one said anything.
   We knew everything.

   _____

3. We opened a window.
   A bird flew in.

   _____

4. Seth jogs every morning.
   His wife swims every afternoon.

   _____

GO ON TO THE NEXT PAGE

5. Write down everything.
We will forget to buy something.

DIRECT QUOTATIONS

Write these direct quotations correctly.

1. Herbert asked why are you doing that?

_____

2. Florence asked who is going to the party tomorrow?

_____

3. I asked what are you doing later?

_____

4. Mateo asked is that the truth?

_____

5. Julia asked did you do that?

_____

DIRECT AND INDIRECT QUOTATIONS

The following sentences contain direct quotations. Write each sentence over so that it contains an indirect quotation.

1. Berta said, "I need more time to do that."

_____

2. Jane said, "I am happy about this."

_____

3. Maria said, "David has everything he needs."

_____

4. Laurent said, "Tara is a lovely young woman."

_____

5. Larry said, "I like working here."

_____

GO ON TO THE NEXT PAGE

END MARKS (PUNCTUATION)
Put the correct end mark at the end of each sentence.

1. Are you really going to do that

2. He asked whether you were going to do that

3. I asked him if he knew what time it was

4. How late are you

5. Did you ask if he will attend the meeting

THE PRONOUNS *WHO*, *WHOM*, AND *WHOSE*
Fill in each blank with **who**, **whom**, or **whose**.

1. Is that about _____ I think it is?

2. _____ party is this?

3. For _____ did you buy this?

4. _____ said that?

5. With _____ are you going?

USING THE WORDS *HAS* AND *HAVE* WITH VERBS
Fill in each blank with the correct verb or verb phrase.

1. We _____ there before. (**have gone** or **went**)

2. Carol _____ many people for a long time. (**has helped** or **helped**)

3. John _____ many interesting people in the past few years.
   (**has met** or **met**)

4. We _____ her for years. (**have known** or **knew**)

5. The snake _____ the man's leg earlier. (**has bitten** or **bit**)

ADDING *ING* TO VERBS WITH A HELPING VERB
In each blank, write the verb phrase that describes action that is going on right now.

1. Sharon _____ a book. (**write**)

2. We _____ away soon. (**go**)

3. They _____ home. (**stay**)

GO ON TO THE NEXT PAGE

4. My friends _____ cards today. (**play**)

5. Ben _____ his truck tonight. (**drive**)

THE VERB *BE*

Fill in each blank with **was**, **were**, **has been**, or **have been**.

1. I _____ here for a long time.

2. We _____ there yesterday.

3. She _____ away for weeks.

4. The workers _____ busy for hours now.

5. He _____ very tired earlier.

THE VERBS *FORGET, FORGETS, FORGOT, WILL FORGET,* AND *FORGOTTEN*

Fill in the blanks with **forget**, **forgets**, **forgot**, **will forget**, or **forgotten**.

1. I _____ to bring the book you wanted.

2. He has _____ almost everything.

3. Victoria _____ by tomorrow.

4. Laura _____ lots of things now.

5. They _____ their lunches yesterday.

SPELLING

Use each of the following words in a sentence.

1. vegetables

_____

2. marriage

_____

3. written

_____

4. Thursday

_____

5. sincerely

_____

GO ON TO THE NEXT PAGE

ALPHABETIZING (USING THE DICTIONARY)

Use the guide words **short** and **shrimp** to answer these questions. Write **Yes** or **No** in each blank.

1. Is the word **sharp** on this page? _____

2. Is the word **shrill** on this page? _____

3. Is the word **shrine** on this page? _____

4. Is the word **shoe** on this page? _____

5. Is the word **shore** on this page? _____

STOP CHECK ANSWERS BEGINNING ON PAGE 148.

Count how many items you answered correctly in each **Section** of the Chapter Five Review. Write your score per section in the **My Scores** column. If all of your section scores are as high as the **Good Scores**, take the Posttest. If any of your section scores are lower than the **Good Scores**, study the lessons on the assigned **Review Pages** again before you take the Posttest.

Section	Good Scores	My Scores	Review Pages
Capitalizing (Common Nouns and Proper Nouns)	8, 9, or 10		100
Combining Sentences	4 or 5		101
Combining Sentences	4 or 5		102
Combining Sentences	4 or 5		103
Direct Quotations	4 or 5		104–105
Direct and Indirect Quotations	4 or 5		106
End Marks (Punctuation)	4 or 5		107
The Pronouns **Who**, **Whom**, and **Whose**	4 or 5		108
Using the Words **Has** and **Have** with Verbs	4 or 5		109
Adding **ing** to Verbs with a Helping Verb	4 or 5		110
The Verb **Be**	4 or 5		111
The Verbs **Forget**, **Forgets**, **Forgot**, **Will Forget**, and **Forgotten**	4 or 5		112
Spelling	4 or 5		113
Alphabetizing (Using the Dictionary)	4 or 5		114

CAPITALIZING

Correct the following nouns that are capitalized incorrectly. Put a **C** in the blank by those that are correct.

1. apple   _____
2. lincoln center   _____
3. Marshal company   _____
4. senator   _____
5. aunt sharon   _____

6. general grant   _____
7. daughter   _____
8. manager   _____
9. mother   _____
10. dentist   _____

SINGULAR AND PLURAL SUBJECTS

Underline the nouns and pronouns in the complete subjects of each of the following sentences. Write **S** in the blank if the subject of the sentence is singular. Write **P** in the blank if the subject of the sentence is plural.

1. My teacher is very pretty.   _____
2. That noise drives me crazy.   _____
3. My problems caused me to drop out of school.   _____
4. My boyfriends are always at our house.   _____
5. My parents live with us.   _____

AGREEMENT OF SUBJECT AND VERB

Underline the verb that is correct for each sentence.

1. My teacher's voice (**is** or **are**) very pleasant.
2. The school's teachers (**is** or **are**) all very nice.
3. One man's wife (**come** or **comes**) to class with him.
4. Jane's boyfriend (**drive** or **drives**) her to school.
5. The school's guards (**protects** or **protect**) us at night.

GO ON TO THE NEXT PAGE

COMBINING SENTENCES

Write one sentence that combines all the sentences in each set.

1. Luis has his own bowling ball.
   Jane has her own bowling ball.
   Claire has her own bowling ball.

   _____

   _____

2. Gregorio wants his own car now.
   Hiro wants his own car now.
   Choi wants her own car now.

   _____

   _____

3. Roberto wants his own business soon.
   Pierre wants his own business soon.
   Mary wants her own business soon.

   _____

   _____

4. Georgio has changed his mind again.
   Judit has changed her mind again.
   Keung has changed his mind again.

   _____

   _____

5. Tim is still looking for his dream mate.
   James is still looking for his dream mate.
   Diane is still looking for her dream mate.

   _____

   _____

GO ON TO THE NEXT PAGE

COMBINING SENTENCES

Write one sentence that combines the two in each of the following pairs. Use a comma with **or**, **but**, or **and** in the sentence you write.

1. Life is more difficult today.
   It is also more exciting.

   _____

2. Some of my friends finished school.
   They have good jobs.

   _____

3. I dropped out of school.
   Now no one will hire me.

   _____

4. I have to do something with my life.
   It is hard to know what to do.

   _____

5. I must get a decent job.
   My wife will leave me.

   _____

COMBINING SENTENCES

For each of the following combinations, write a sentence over if it is not correct. Write a **C** in the blank following sentence combinations that are correct.

1. It's hard going back to school, but I am doing it.

   _____

2. Everyone is very helpful, they want me to get ahead.

   _____

3. My wife is supporting me, she wants me to do well.

   _____

4. I am trying hard, but it's not easy.

   _____

5. We are in this together, we will make it.

   _____

GO ON TO THE NEXT PAGE

DIRECT QUOTATIONS

Write these direct quotations correctly.

1. Jeff's friend asked is it time to go yet?

   _____

2. Maria asked why does this cost so much?

   _____

3. José said everything seems to cost a lot.

   _____

4. Joseph said that person looks odd.

   _____

5. Paula asked did the police catch the robber?

   _____

DIRECT AND INDIRECT QUOTATIONS

The following sentences contain direct quotations. Write each sentence over so that it contains an indirect quotation.

1. Franco said, "I need more time to finish the work."

   _____

2. Luisa said, "This has been a good year for me."

   _____

3. Mei said, "The storekeeper charged me too much."

   _____

4. Harry said, "My children need many things."

   _____

5. Anthony said, "Jerry is my best friend."

   _____

GO ON TO THE NEXT PAGE

THE PRONOUNS *ANYBODY, ANYONE, EVERYBODY, EVERYONE, NOBODY, NO ONE, SOMEBODY,* AND *SOMEONE*

Underline the verb that is correct for the sentence.

1. Someone (**is** or **are**) playing a joke on us.

2. Anybody (**is** or **are**) able to do that.

3. Everyone (**need** or **needs**) someone.

4. Nobody (**has** or **have**) a chance here.

5. Everybody (**cry** or **cries**) at that movie.

PRONOUNS (SHOWING OWNERSHIP OR BELONGING TO)

Fill in each blank correctly with a pronoun that shows ownership.

1. These are Donna's children.

   The children are _____ .

   These are _____ children.

2. Robert's wife is nice.

   _____ wife is nice.

3. The bird's leg is hurt.

   _____ leg is hurt.

4. The women's meeting is tomorrow.

   _____ meeting is tomorrow.

5. These are the children's books.

   These are _____ .

   These are _____ books.

PRONOUNS AND WHAT THEY REFER TO

Fill in each blank with the correct pronoun. The pronoun should refer to the subject of the sentence.

1. The cute little rabbit ate _____ carrot.

2. Jack drank _____ milk.

3. Herb and Kim ate _____ dinner.

4. Sharon does _____ exercises every day.

5. Carol, John, and Seth ride _____ bikes every day.

GO ON TO THE NEXT PAGE

THE PRONOUNS *WHO, WHOM,* AND *WHOSE*

Fill in each blank with **who**, **whom**, or **whose**.

1. For _____ do you work?

2. _____ said those cruel words?

3. To _____ are you sending that?

4. _____ house is this?

5. _____ is going with us?

END MARKS (PUNCTUATION)

Put the proper end mark at the end of each sentence.

1. They asked when we arrived yesterday

2. James said he knows about Gil and Elena

3. Who refused the invitation

4. She asked if they could stay a little longer

5. This is an incredible view

ADJECTIVES

Fill in each blank with the correct adjective.

1. Jane gives the _____ parties. (**good, better,** or **best**)

2. Fred drank _____ beer than you. (**many, more,** or **most**)

3. Yesterday was a _____ day. (**good, better,** or **best**)

4. Maria likes this _____ than that. (**good, better,** or **best**)

5. This report is _____ than the other. (**bad, worse,** or **worst**)

REGULAR AND IRREGULAR VERBS

In the blank, write the form of each verb that shows action in the past.

REGULAR VERBS		IRREGULAR VERBS	
1. stay	_____	6. forget	_____
2. try	_____	7. go	_____
3. clean	_____	8. take	_____
4. seem	_____	9. run	_____
5. walk	_____	10. do	_____

GO ON TO THE NEXT PAGE

THE VERBS *CATCH*, *CATCHES*, *CAUGHT*, AND *WILL CATCH*

Fill in each blank with **catch**, **catches**, **caught**, or **will catch**.

1. I _____ his cold this morning.

2. Those campers _____ raccoons wherever they camp.

3. The police _____ the robber soon.

4. My boyfriend _____ for a baseball team now.

5. We _____ lots of fish tomorrow.

USING THE WORDS *HAS* AND *HAVE* WITH VERBS

Fill in each blank with the correct verb or verb phrase.

1. They _____ there often. (**fished** or **have fished**)

2. We _____ here for days. (**were** or **have been**)

3. I _____ her yesterday. (**saw** or **have seen**)

4. The twins _____ a new place last week.

   (**opened** or **have opened**)

5. Julio _____ well with his family for years.

   (**worked** or **has worked**)

ADDING *ING* TO VERBS WITH A HELPING VERB

In each blank, write the verb phrase that describes action that is going on right now.

1. Florence _____ dinner for us. (**make**)

2. Terry _____ his father's business. (**run**)

3. My boyfriend _____ now. (**work**)

4. My parents _____ apart from each other. (**live**)

5. We _____ to make the best of it. (**try**)

GO ON TO THE NEXT PAGE

THE VERB *BE*

Fill in each blank with **am**, **is**, **are**, **was**, **were**, **will be**, **has been**, or **have been**.

1. It _____ hard to be a parent now.

2. Drugs and alcohol _____ big problems at this time.

3. It _____ a difficult year so far.

4. Diane _____ in trouble at school yesterday.

5. We _____ happy to see her teacher tomorrow.

THE VERBS *FORGET, FORGETS, FORGOT, WILL FORGET,* AND *FORGOTTEN*

Fill in each blank with **forget**, **forgets**, **forgot**, **will forget**, or **forgotten**.

1. My son _____ my birthday yesterday.

2. I _____ many things lately.

3. My husband and I _____ each others birthdays a few times now.

4. He _____ all about that in time.

5. I _____ things all the time.

ADVERBS

In each blank, write the comparing form of the adverb correctly.

1. Henry walks _____ than Jill. (**fast**)

2. She has worked the _____ of all of us. (**steadily**)

3. Jerry is _____ of himself than you are. (**sure**)

4. James drives _____ than Kenneth. (**carefully**)

5. The children are playing _____ now than before. (**quietly**)

THE WORDS *WELL, BETTER,* AND *BEST*

Fill in each blank with the correct form of the word **well**.

1. Florence is the _____ at dealing with people.

2. Jennifer does _____ in school.

3. Tina reads and writes the _____ in her class.

4. Hiromi runs _____ than his friend Terry.

5. Gary, Donna, and Laura play _____ together.

GO ON TO THE NEXT PAGE

SHOWING OWNERSHIP OR BELONGING TO (POSSESSION)

For each of the following nouns, write the form that shows ownership.

1. fox _____
2. James _____
3. shelves _____
4. mice _____
5. knife _____

6. class _____
7. wolf _____
8. girls _____
9. shirt _____
10. children _____

THE COMMA

Each of the following sentences has two adjectives. Add commas between adjectives where they are needed. If a sentence needs no comma, write **NC** in the blank.

1. My beautiful new dress is ruined. _____
2. This yellow blouse is dirty. _____
3. My cat wears a pretty blue coat in the winter. _____
4. At the shelter there were tired hungry people. _____
5. I love this soft fluffy blanket. _____

CONTRACTIONS

There are two contractions in each of these sentences. Each of the contractions stands for two words. Write those two words in the blanks below the sentences.

1. He's a good worker, but she's shown a negative attitude toward him.

   _____ _____

2. I'll be there, but he's not able to accept the invitation.

   _____ _____

3. I'm glad that we're friends.

   _____ _____

4. It's a shame that they've had so many problems with their son.

   _____ _____

5. He'll be able to pick it up if you're not able to do so.

   _____ _____

GO ON TO THE NEXT PAGE

THE WORDS *A* AND *AN*
Put **a** or **an** before each of the following.

1. _____ elevator   6. _____ home

2. _____ odor   7. _____ uncle

3. _____ hospital   8. _____ family

4. _____ year   9. _____ union card

5. _____ hour   10. _____ honest person

WRITING AN INVITATION
Write a letter to invite a friend to an anniversary party.

_____

_____

_____

_____

_____

_____

_____

_____

GO ON TO THE NEXT PAGE

WRITING A BUSINESS LETTER

Write a business letter to answer an ad for a job as short-order cook. Write to **Frank Galillio, Galillio's Restaurant, 214 Derby Road, Los Angeles, California 91354**.

SPELLING

The following words are spelled incorrectly. Spell them correctly.

1. untill _____
2. holliday _____
3. thankgiving _____
4. looce _____
5. enugh _____
6. neice _____
7. sience _____
8. sincerly _____
9. writen _____
10. finaly _____
11. favrite _____
12. plese _____
13. quiette _____
14. exellent _____
15. beggining _____
16. turky _____
17. sentense _____
18. marrage _____
19. thurday _____
20. vegtables _____

ALPHABETIZING (USING THE PHONE BOOK)

Use the guide names **Mendez** and **Minor** to answer the questions. Write **Yes** or **No** in each blank.

1. Is the name **Ramon Meldez** on this page? _____
2. Is the name **Harry Miers** on this page? _____
3. Is the name **Mary Mertz** on this page? _____
4. Is the name **William Miser** on this page? _____
5. Is the name **Robert Meyers** on this page? _____

STOP CHECK ANSWERS BEGINNING ON PAGE 150.

Count how many items you answered correctly in each **Section** of the Posttest. Write your score per section in the **My Scores** column. If all of your section scores are as high as the **Good Scores**, go on to *Power English 7,* Chapter One. If any of your section scores are lower than the **Good Scores**, study the lessons on the assigned **Review Pages** again before you go on to *Power English 7,* Chapter One.

Section	Good Scores	My Scores	Review Pages
Capitalizing	8, 9, or 10		2, 26, 50, 74, 100
Singular and Plural Subjects	4 or 5		3, 51
Agreement of Subject and Verb	4 or 5		27
Combining Sentences	4 or 5		4–7, 28–29, 52–53, 101
Combining Sentences	4 or 5		30–31, 75, 102
Combining Sentences	4 or 5		54–55, 76–77, 103
Direct Quotations	4 or 5		78–79, 104–105
Direct and Indirect Quotations	4 or 5		80–81, 106
The Pronouns **Anybody, Anyone, Everybody, Everyone, Nobody, No One, Somebody,** and **Someone**	4 or 5		32, 56
Pronouns (Showing Ownership or Belonging To)	4 or 5		33–34
Pronouns and What They Refer To	4 or 5		9

Section	Good Scores	My Scores	Review Pages
The Pronouns **Who**, **Whom**, and **Whose**	4 or 5		82, 108
End Marks (Punctuation)	4 or 5		8, 107
Adjectives	4 or 5		10
Regular and Irregular Verbs	8, 9, or 10		11, 35
The Verbs **Catch**, **Catches**, **Caught**, and **Will Catch**	4 or 5		57
Using the Words **Has** and **Have** with Verbs	4 or 5		58–61, 83, 109
Adding **ing** to Verbs with a Helping Verb	4 or 5		62, 84, 110
The Verb **Be**	4 or 5		63, 111
The Verbs **Forget**, **Forgets**, **Forgot**, **Will Forget**, and **Forgotten**	4 or 5		112
Adverbs	4 or 5		12–13, 85
The Words **Well**, **Better**, and **Best**	4 or 5		36
Showing Ownership or Belonging To (Possession)	8, 9, or 10		14, 37
The Comma	4 or 5		86
Contractions	4 or 5		64
The Words **A** and **An**	8, 9, or 10		87
Writing an Invitation	A correct letter		15–16
Writing a Business Letter	A correct letter		38–39, 88
Spelling	16–20		17, 40, 65, 89, 113
Alphabetizing (Using the Phone Book)	4 or 5		41, 66

ANSWERS

Chapter One
Capitalizing (Movie and TV Show Titles) (p. 2)

1. My favorite movie is still <u>Casablanca</u> with Humphrey Bogart.
2. Johnny Carson is the host of "The Tonight Show" on NBC.
3. Ronald Reagan was in the film <u>King's Row</u>.
4. Like many books, <u>From Here to Eternity</u> became a movie.
5. In March I read George Orwell's <u>Animal Farm</u> again.

Singular and Plural Subjects (p. 3)

You should have a line under the following.

1. people (P)
2. brother (S)
3. Bill, I (P)
4. idea (S)
5. divorce (S)
6. parents (P)
7. Frank, Kathy (P)
8. They (P)
9. children (P)
10. It (S)

Combining Sentences (pp. 4–5)

1. Marie, José, and Mike are eating their breakfasts.
2. Charles, Jim, and I go to our clubs on Saturdays.
3. My father, my mother, and I like our gifts.
4. George, Pat, and Kim ride their bikes to work every day.
5. My bird and cat play with their toys.

Combining Sentences (pp. 6–7)

1. Grant, Keung, and Barney are starting their new jobs today.
2. Teresa and Ben use their credit cards too much.
3. The cat, Wayne, and Jessie drink milk every day.
4. Henri, Pina, and Ali put their houses on the market today.
5. Eleni, Ann, and Diego buy their groceries every day.

End Marks (Punctuation) (p. 8)

1. Whose dog is that?
2. That is incredible news!
3. Who is going to the movies?
4. Please move.
5. Grab that person.
   or: Grab that person!
6. He looks happy.
7. You look fantastic!
8. Slow down when you come to curves.
9. Please share these.
10. How many people will be here today?

Pronouns and What They Refer To (p. 9)

1. her
2. his
3. their
4. my
5. its
6. its
7. our
8. their
9. his
10. their

Adjectives (p. 10)

1. best
2. many
3. worse
4. worst
5. better
6. most
7. best
8. good
9. more
10. best

Regular and Irregular Verbs (p. 11)

1. played
2. jumped
3. went
4. did
5. learned
6. ate
7. helped
8. stopped
9. had
10. began

Adverbs (p. 12)

1. faster
2. more harshly
3. more rudely
4. more carefully
5. more cheaply
6. louder **or** more loudly
7. oftener **or** more often
8. more brightly
9. more rapidly
10. harder

Adverbs (p. 13)

1. loudest
2. most slowly
3. craziest
4. longest
5. most carefully
6. most furiously
7. most quickly
8. most clearly
9. rudest
10. steadiest

Showing Ownership or Belonging To (Possession) (p. 14)

1. boss's
2. Andrew's
3. shelves'
4. Mrs. Brown's
5. father's
6. baby's
7. women's
8. Jeff's
9. children's
10. peaches'

Writing an Invitation (pp. 15–16)

Sample letter:

December 15, 1990

Dear Oscar and Gloria,

We are having a New Year's Eve Party at our home on December 31 and would like you to come. It will begin about 9:00 P.M.

Everyone is bringing a special dish to the party. Please phone to let us know if you will be with us this New Year's Eve.

Fondly,
Teruo and Matsue

Spelling (p. 17)

Sample answers:
1. (until)   We can't do anything until they arrive.
2. (loose)   Are those pants too loose on you?
3. (through) I am through with them after today.
4. (please)   Please don't go yet.
5. (quiet)   Be quiet!

Alphabetizing (Using the Dictionary) (p. 18)

1. Yes
2. Yes
3. No
4. Yes
5. Yes
6. Yes
7. Yes
8. No
9. Yes
10. Yes

Chapter One Review
Capitalizing (Movie and TV Show Titles) (p. 19)

1. The Color Purple with Whoopi Goldberg and Oprah Winfrey is an excellent movie that takes place in the South.
2. The film Fatal Attraction is a thrilling movie.
3. Empire of the Sun is a film about the Japanese in Shanghai in World War II.
4. Cry Freedom is a film based on the life of Stephen Biko, a black activist.
5. The old "Father Knows Best" with Robert Young was a family television show.

Singular and Plural Subjects (p. 19)

You should have a line under the following.
1. men (P)
2. They (P)
3. sister; brother (P)
4. dealer (S)
5. brothers (P)

Combining Sentences (p. 20)

1. James, Clara, and Felipe are taking their vacations soon.
2. The cat, dog, and hamster are eating now.
3. Jane, Brigitte, and I love our new apartments.
4. Larry and Betty enjoy their jobs.
5. Franco, Michel, and Antonio are working on their own.

End Marks (Punctuation) (p. 20)

1. Are you sure he will be there?
2. No, I can't go.
3. This is really great!
4. How much should I pay for it?
5. I like her a lot.

Pronouns and What They Refer To (p. 21)

1. her
2. their
3. our
4. my
5. its

Adjectives (p. 21)

1. best
2. better
3. worst
4. more
5. most

Regular and Irregular Verbs (p. 21)

1. drank
2. played
3. did
4. danced
5. knew
6. got
7. helped
8. had
9. went
10. was

Adverbs (p. 22)

1. more carefully
2. more rapidly
3. loudest
4. most swiftly
5. more angrily

Showing Ownership or Belonging To (Possession) (p. 22)

1. Hideo's
2. Claude's
3. wife's
4. women's
5. Pappases'

Writing an Invitation (p. 22)

Sample letter:

> February 11, 1990
>
> Dear Rosa,
>
> Carlos and I are giving a surprise anniversary party for Jean and George. The party will be at our home on Saturday, February 27, at 8:30 P.M. We hope you will help us celebrate. Please phone by February 21 to tell us if you can make it.
>
> Fondly,
> Mercedes

Spelling (p. 23)

Sample answers:
1. I will wait until it gets dark.
2. These clothes are too loose on me.
3. After today I am through with smoking.
4. Please stay here with us.
5. You must be more quiet.

Alphabetizing (Using the Dictionary) (p. 23)

1. Yes   2. Yes   3. No   4. No   5. No

Chapter Two
Capitalizing (Names of Companies) (p. 26)

1. Mr. Grant works for the ABC Motor Company in Maine.
2. George, Frank, and I work for a computer company called Computer World.
3. I am a carpenter and work for Atlas Building Company.
4. Nick and Tony are waiters at Club Happiness.
5. The banker at National Bank lives in Oakland, California.
6. A new French cook starts work at the Paradise Restaurant in May.
7. Aunt Sara and Uncle Bill own the Capital Laundry Service.
8. Miss Sanchez quit her job at the Corbett Ford Company.
9. I brought my car to the Fix Everything Garage on Main Street.
10. Mr. and Mrs. Holly started work at the Limited Express Company last Tuesday.

Agreement of Subject and Verb (p. 27)

You should have a line under the following.
1. are
2. is
3. visit
4. is
5. barks
6. has
7. are
8. look
9. needs
10. talk

Combining Sentences (p. 28)

1. Mallory plays the piano well, and he performs for his friends.
2. Keith is retired, and he stays home most of the time.
3. Mildred works nine months a year, and she has the summer off.
4. Their house is in Brooklyn, and it is rather old.
5. The park is nearby, and it is often crowded with people.

Combining Sentences (p. 29)

1. She makes a lot of money and goes on many free trips.
2. David is running for City Council and needs a lot of votes to win.
3. The present councilman wants to stay in office and is campaigning.
4. The voters want a change and need someone they can trust.
5. The election is in three days and promises to be very exciting.

Combining Sentences (pp. 30–31)

1. Fumiko has a new job, and she is moving to Chicago.
   Fumiko has a new job and is moving to Chicago.
2. Mrs. Wong just bought a new car, and she is going away on vacation.
   Mrs. Wong just bought a new car and is going away on vacation.
3. Ms. Davis plays tennis, and she wins many matches.
   Ms. Davis plays tennis and wins many matches.
4. Isabel wants to be an actress, and she is going to acting school.
   Isabel wants to be an actress and is going to acting school.
5. Scott's house is not too large, and it needs many repairs.
   Scott's house is not too large and needs many repairs.

The Pronouns *Anyone, Everyone, No One,* and *Someone* (p. 32)

You should have underlined the following.

1. puts	5. cries	8. feels
2. has	6. is	9. likes
3. plays	7. is	10. remembers
4. wants		

Pronouns (Showing Ownership or Belonging To) (pp. 33–34)

1. mine	6. her
2. its	7. hers; her
3. their; theirs	8. Her
4. Her	9. His
5. His	10. Its

Regular and Irregular Verbs (p. 35)

1. tried	5. washed	8. knew
2. trained	6. ran	9. drank
3. showed	7. got	10. went
4. spied		

The Words *Well, Better,* and *Best* (p. 36)

1. better	5. best	8. best
2. better	6. best	9. better
3. best	7. better	10. well
4. well		

Showing Ownership or Belonging To (Possession) (p. 37)

1. men's	5. sofa's	8. class's
2. calf's	6. homes'	9. dresses'
3. mice's	7. babies'	10. witch's
4. drape's		

Writing a Business Letter (pp. 38–39)

21 Davis Boulevard
Chicago, Illinois 60624
June 6, 1990

Felix Garza
ABC Chemical Company
43 Second Avenue
Chicago, Illinois 60624

Dear Mr. Garza:

The chemicals I purchased from you for my lawn ruined it. Please contact me immediately to discuss this.

Sincerely yours,
Greg Harper

Spelling (p. 40)

Sample answers:
1. (Thanksgiving)   I had a lot to be grateful for last Thanksgiving.
2. (holiday)   What holiday do you like best?
3. (favorite)   My favorite holiday is Thanksgiving.
4. (turkey)   I love to eat turkey.
5. (together)   I love to be together with my family.

Alphabetizing (Using the Dictionary) (p. 41)

1. No	3. No	5. No	7. No	9. No
2. Yes	4. No	6. No	8. No	10. No

Chapter Two Review
Capitalizing (Names of Companies) (p. 42)

1. My Aunt Nancy works at the ABC Clothing Company.
2. I am going west to begin work at the Expert Computer Company.
3. Do you work at Burger Delight?
4. Jim Haines is a salesman at George's Furniture Company.
5. I'm a carpenter at Drake Construction Company.

Agreement of Subject and Verb (p. 42)

You should have a line under the following.
1. is   3. look   5. have
2. do   4. are

Combining Sentences (pp. 42–43)

1. Many drug addicts live on my street, and they sell drugs to young children.
   Many drug addicts live on my street and sell drugs to young children.
2. Parents fear for their children's lives, and they don't know what to do.
   Parents fear for their children's lives and don't know what to do.
3. The schools aren't safe from drugs, and they have many drug dealers on their grounds.
   The schools aren't safe from drugs and have many drug dealers on their grounds.
4. Some children as young as ten are on drugs, and they do not attend school.
   Some children as young as ten are on drugs and do not attend school.
5. The police should do more about drugs in schools, and they should rid our schools of drug dealers.
   The police should do more about drugs in schools and should rid our schools of drug dealers.

The Pronouns *Anyone, Everyone, No One*, and *Someone* (p. 43)

1. is   3. has   5. knows
2. is   4. has

Pronouns (Showing Ownership or Belonging To) (pp. 43–44)

1. hers   3. his   5. Its
2. mine   4. their

Regular and Irregular Verbs (p. 44)

1. bit   5. joined   8. drank
2. tried   6. did   9. worked
3. began   7. stayed   10. ate
4. went

The Words *Well, Better*, and *Best* (p. 44)

1. better   4. better
2. best   5. well, better, **or** best
3. well, better, **or** best

Showing Ownership or Belonging To (Possession) (p. 44)

1. children's   6. mouse's
2. James's   7. church's
3. flower's   8. box's
4. wages'   9. doctor's
5. ladies'   10. wives'

Writing a Business Letter (p. 45)

214 Morris Avenue
New York, New York 10022
May 27, 1990

Walter Jackson
Forbes Clothing Outlet
453 Center Street
New York, New York 10003

Dear Mr. Jackson:

  I ordered two pairs of work pants from you over two months ago. I still have not received them. If I do not receive them soon, I will cancel my order.

     Yours truly,
     Benjamin Helms

Spelling (p. 46)

Sample answers:
1. Next Thanksgiving will be our best one.
2. Thanksgiving is a wonderful holiday.
3. It is our favorite holiday.
4. We always have turkey on Thanksgiving.
5. Thanksgiving is a time for families and friends to be together.

Alphabetizing (Using the Dictionary) (p. 46)

1. Yes   2. No   3. No   4. Yes   5. Yes

Chapter Three
Capitalizing (Names of Buildings) (p. 50)

1. I went to Shea Stadium to see a baseball game.
2. Faye saw the Empire State Building when she went to New York.
3. The National Bank is on Center Street in Ohio.
4. Mrs. Trent sang at Carnegie Hall when she was younger.
5. Ed and I are going west to California to visit the Coliseum.
6. My English friend visited the World Trade Center in February.
7. His Uncle Max and I went to the Sears Tower in Chicago.
8. Ben went to the Drake Building on Foster Street.
9. In May Don is going south to Florida to visit Disney World.
10. Molly was going west to Seattle, Washington, to see the Kingdome.

Singular and Plural Subjects (p. 51)

You should have a line under the following.
1. parents (P)
2. home (S)
3. dogs (P)
4. children (P)
5. son, daughter (P)
6. wife (S)
7. friends (P)
8. aunt (S)
9. sleeve (S)
10. supper (S)

Combining Sentences (p. 52)

1. The young bride left home one night, and her husband never saw her again.
2. She went for a walk late at night, and her husband stayed behind.
3. People searched everywhere for her, and the police questioned everyone.
4. Everyone feared the worst, and sometime later her body was found.
5. The young bride had been murdered, and the police suspected the husband.

Combining Sentences (p. 53)

1. Today's single people have many concerns, and one of them is fear of AIDS.
2. Some famous people died of AIDS, and that helped give the disease national attention.
3. AIDS has spread widely, and casual sex can be dangerous.
4. Young people need to know about AIDS, and schools have begun to teach them.
5. Many young women today want good, strong relationships, and many young men desire the same.

Combining Sentences (pp. 54–55)

1. Jeff's dog is lost, and it has been missing for two days.
   Jeff's dog is lost and has been missing for two days.
2. Jeff's neighbors are looking for the dog, and they are searching everywhere.
   Jeff's neighbors are looking for the dog and are searching everywhere.
3. Betty's husband just had a heart attack, and he is not doing well.
   Betty's husband just had a heart attack and is not doing well.
4. Daniella's uncle is retiring soon, and he is moving to another state.
   Daniella's uncle is retiring soon and is moving to another state.
5. Nader's brother was in an accident, and he was badly hurt.
   Nader's brother was in an accident and was badly hurt.

The Pronouns *Anybody, Everybody, Nobody,* and *Somebody* (p. 56)

You should have a line under the following:
1. is
2. needs
3. has
4. talks
5. plays
6. stays
7. has
8. knows
9. is
10. wants

The Verbs *Catch, Catches, Caught,* and *Will Catch* (p. 57)

1. caught
2. will catch
3. catches
4. caught
5. will catch
6. catches
7. caught
8. catch
9. catches
10. caught

Using the Words *Has* and *Have* with Verbs (pp. 58–59)

1. have started
2. tried
3. moved
4. have looked
5. rushed
6. baked
7. traveled
8. has played
9. have worked
10. tripped

Using the Words *Has* and *Have* with Verbs (pp. 60–61)

1. have needed
2. have run
3. sold
4. showed
5. caught
6. played
7. invited
8. have spent
9. has wanted
10. earned

Adding *ing* to Verbs with a Helping Verb (p. 62)

1. is talking
2. is trying
3. is mowing
4. are eating
5. are traveling
6. is buying
7. am gaining
8. are planning
9. is growing
10. is leaving

The Verb *Be* (p. 63)

1. will be
2. were
3. am **or** am being
4. were
5. have been
6. has been
7. have been
8. was
9. will be
10. has been

Contractions (p. 64)

1. I have; I am
2. She is; it will
3. They are; they will
4. I will; you will
5. They have; I have

Spelling (p. 65)

Sample answers:
1. (enough)   We have had enough of this.
2. (beginning)   Please start at the beginning.
3. (heard)   Have you heard from her yet?
4. (later)   It is later than you think.
5. (sentence)   Did you write this sentence?

Alphabetizing (Using the Phone Book) (p. 66)

1. No   3. Yes   5. Yes   7. No   9. No
2. No   4. Yes   6. No   8. Yes   10. No

Chapter Three Review
Capitalizing (Names of Buildings) (p. 67)

1. Aunt Diane and Uncle Elton go to the Metrodome in Minneapolis to watch football games.
2. Mr. Carter, my father, and I go to Yankee Stadium to watch baseball games.
3. Have you ever been to the Astrodome in Houston, Texas?
4. No, I've only been to the Superdome in New Orleans, Louisiana.
5. The Kennedy Center for Performing Arts is in Washington, D.C.

Singular and Plural Subjects (p. 67)

You should have a line under the following.
1. parents (P)
2. wife (S)
3. apartment (S)
4. children (P)
5. bark (S)

Combining Sentences (pp. 67–68)

1. The snowstorm is over, and the damage has to be repaired.
2. Bob just got a promotion, and his girlfriend found a good job.
3. I lost my watch yesterday, and my wife lost hers today.
4. The tickets to the show will cost a lot, and we will still not have good seats.
5. I don't like meat, and my boyfriend doesn't like vegetables.

Combining Sentences (pp. 68–69)

1. Sam's work is very important, and it requires long hours at the job.
   Sam's work is very important and requires long hours at the job.
2. John could stay longer, and he could eat dinner with us.
   John could stay longer and eat dinner with us.
3. Tuesday was a stormy day, and it was not a good day to go out.
   Tuesday was a stormy day and was not a good day to go out.
4. Sherry is an excellent supervisor, and she has a group of loyal employees.
   Sherry is an excellent supervisor and has a group of loyal employees.
5. Mr. Veldez is traveling alone, and he has no baggage.
   Mr. Veldez is traveling alone and has no baggage.

The Pronouns *Anybody, Everybody, Nobody,* and *Somebody* (p. 69)

1. is
2. has
3. is
4. likes
5. knows

The Verbs *Catch, Catches, Caught,* and *Will Catch* (p. 69)

1. will catch
2. catches
3. caught
4. Catch
5. caught

Using the Words *Has* and *Have* with Verbs (p. 69)

1. have tried
2. left
3. have traveled
4. has worked
5. played

Adding *ing* to Verbs with a Helping Verb (p. 70)

1. is going
2. am feeling
3. is trying
4. are keeping
5. are supporting

The Verb *Be* (p. 70)

1. will be
2. have been
3. has been
4. are being
5. were

Contractions (p. 70)

1. I will; I have
2. They will; we will
3. He is; he has
4. We have; we will
5. It has; it is

Spelling (p. 71)

Sample answers:
1. That is enough of that.
2. This is a good beginning for us.
3. Yes, we heard all about it.
4. He will arrive later.
5. Is this sentence correct?

Alphabetizing (Using the Phone Book) (p. 71)

1. No   2. No   3. Yes   4. No   5. Yes

Chapter Four
Capitalizing (Common Nouns and Proper Nouns) (p. 74)

1. Uncle Ramon
2. French
3. Korean War
4. C
5. winter
6. February
7. East Berlin
8. Miami
9. Valentine's Day
10. John L. Sullivan
11. onion
12. cousin
13. C
14. Puerto Rico
15. star
16. C
17. fall
18. summer
19. Ms. Tsu
20. crow

Combining Sentences (p. 75)

1. My husband invited his friend to dinner, but I do not have enough food in the house.
2. My husband should ask me first, but he never does.
3. It makes me very angry, but my husband doesn't seem to care.
4. Now I have to run to the store, but I do not have enough time.
5. I could try to phone my husband, but he probably left work already.

Combining Sentences (pp. 76–77)

1. I hate staying home on a Saturday night, but no one asked me to go out.
2. Some women ask men out, but I just can't seem to do that.
3. Usually I go out with my friends, but tonight they are all busy.
4. I like to go to movies by myself, and I might do that.
5. The night is still young, and I am going to do something exciting.

Direct Quotations (pp. 78–79)

1. He said, "I am happy."
2. Elias said, "Please send this to Olga."
3. Kiyo said, "Hideo and I are going to visit our aunt."
4. Mrs. Matos said, "Teaching is difficult work."
5. Martin said, "My son is a movie star."
6. Bijan said, "This year has been a hard one for me."
7. Mr. Huang said, "Ben's boss is firing him."
8. Miss Moulin said, "Things will get better soon."
9. Ms. Nomura said, "Sally started a silly story about him."
10. Bob said, "The new plant is very nice."

Direct and Indirect Quotations (pp. 80–81)

1. IQ
2. He said, "That is not a nice thing to do."
3. IQ
4. She said, "No, I am not going with you."
5. IQ
6. IQ
7. Henry said, "I want to learn more about this subject."
8. IQ
9. IQ
10. Yasuko said, "Hidori does not want to meet us."

The Pronouns *Who, Whom*, and *Whose* (p. 82)

1. Who	5. whom	8. Whose
2. whom	6. whom	9. Who
3. Whose	7. Whose	10. Whose
4. Who		

Using the Words *Has* and *Have* with Verbs (p. 83)

1. has seen	6. came
2. chose	7. broke
3. broke	8. chose
4. has broken	9. came
5. has written	10. have chosen

Adding *ing* to Verbs with a Helping Verb (p. 84)

1. are thinking	6. are diving
2. is driving	7. are trying
3. is baking	8. are moving
4. are driving	9. is filing
5. is shining	10. is biting

Adverbs (p. 85)

1. more proudly	6. most often **or** oftenest
2. most carefully	7. more swiftly
3. fastest	8. more fiercely
4. more quietly	9. more happily
5. more beautifully	10. louder

The Comma (p. 86)

1. NC
2. NC
3. The sad, sick dog looked at us.
4. The good, kind woman helped us.
5. NC
6. NC
7. NC
8. The hungry, tired hikers returned late.
9. The itchy, rough sweater bothers me.
10. The kind, hardworking woman smiled at me.

The Words *A* or *An* (p. 87)

1. an underweight person	10. an apricot
2. an eager child	11. an owl
3. an unsolved mystery	12. a ruler
4. a yard	13. an early bus
5. an orange	14. a farmer
6. a pie	15. a garden
7. an ice cream pop	16. a hole
8. an hourglass	17. a jar
9. a park bench	18. a yam
	19. a son
	20. an elevator

Writing a Business Letter (p. 88)

Sample letter:

> 710 Madison Avenue
> Cleveland, Ohio 44102
> March 11, 1990
>
> Joan Forbes
> Personnel Manager
> Best Paper Company
> 111 Beaver Street
> Cleveland, Ohio 44101
>
> Dear Mrs. Forbes:
>
> I am applying for the clerk position you advertised in The Globe. I feel that I have the necessary skills to be an excellent file clerk. I am a dependable and hardworking person, and I want to get ahead. I also have references. My home phone number is (213) 555-8754.
>
> Sincerely yours,
> Florio Meldez

Spelling (p. 89)

Sample answers:
1. (excellent) This is an excellent letter.
2. (finally) He finally got it right.
3. (whether) Do you know whether they are going with us?
4. (niece) You have a lovely niece.
5. (science) I am studying science in school.

Alphabetizing (Using the Dictionary) (p. 90)

1. No	3. Yes	5. Yes	7. No	9. Yes
2. Yes	4. No	6. Yes	8. Yes	10. No

Chapter Four Review
Capitalizing (Common Nouns and Proper Nouns) (p. 91)

1. C
2. Miss Ann Maloney
3. Uncle Herbert
4. C
5. news
6. C
7. Disneyland
8. winter
9. C
10. Italian

Combining Sentences (p. 91)

1. The doorbell rang, but nobody was there.
2. The doctors did not expect the boy to live, but his parents felt there was still a chance.
3. The plane landed safely, but the passengers were still very frightened.
4. Pablo and Marco went hunting, but we decided to stay home.
5. Ramona and Matsue worked hard all day, but their friends went to the beach.

Combining Sentences (p. 92)

1. The sky was cloudy, but it didn't rain.
2. Jane is an excellent student, but her sister Mary does not do well in school.
3. My brother is dating my best girlfriend, and my sister is dating my best friend's brother.
4. She deserves the punishment, but I feel sorry for her.
5. Vacations are my favorite times, and I make the most of them.

Direct Quotations (pp. 92–93)

1. Choi said, "Hold this for me until later."
2. She said, "The movers are coming soon."
3. I said, "Don't go there yet."
4. He said, "The new owners seem to be nice people."
5. Fabio said, "This is the last time we move."

Direct and Indirect Quotations (p. 93)

1. IQ
2. He said, "I can't wait to start work tomorrow."
3. IQ
4. IQ
5. His friend said, "Good Luck on your new job tomorrow."

The Pronouns Who, Whom, and Whose (p. 93)

1. whom
2. whom
3. whose
4. Who
5. Whose

Using the Words Has and Have with Verbs (pp. 93–94)

1. have done
2. has gone
3. wrote
4. caught
5. has invited

Adding ing to Verbs with a Helping Verb (p. 94)

1. is thinking
2. is looking
3. is trying
4. is staying
5. is starving

Adverbs (p. 94)

1. more kindly
2. more quickly
3. more carefully
4. most proudly
5. slowest

The Comma (p. 94)

1. NC
2. The dirty, angry animal growled at us.
3. NC
4. Her cheerful, beautiful sister is here.
5. This is a nice, homey place.

The Words *A* or *An* (p. 95)

1. an ash tray
2. an airline pilot
3. a homely person
4. a handsome man
5. an ill child
6. an open window
7. a color
8. a gorgeous woman
9. an unusual day
10. an errand

Writing a Business Letter (p. 95)

Sample letter:

> 42 Beach Road
> Chicago, Illinois 60641
> May 4, 1990
>
> Michale Mahoney, Manager
> Great Food Stores
> 121 Main Street
> Chicago, Illinois 60653
>
> Dear Mr. Mahoney:
>
> I read your ad in the Chicago Sun and would like to apply for the cashier position. I am very honest, dependable, courteous, hardworking, and friendly. I know that you would be very happy with me. I also have many references. My home phone number is (607) 555-7134.
>
> Sincerely yours,
> Mary Brown

Spelling (p. 96)

Sample answers:
1. You are an excellent worker.
2. Did you finally finish your work?
3. He wants to know whether he is invited.
4. She is my niece.
5. Are you interested in science?

Alphabetizing (Using the Dictionary) (p. 96)

1. No   2. Yes   3. No   4. No   5. No

Chapter Five
Capitalizing (Common Nouns and Proper Nouns) (p. 100)

1. XYZ Company
2. Italy
3. C
4. C
5. C
6. Ms. Veldez
7. hospital
8. C
9. Halloween
10. Mother Maria
11. C
12. C
13. tennis
14. North America
15. C
16. C
17. C
18. English
19. Mercy Hospital
20. C

Combining Sentences (p. 101)

1. I enjoy going out, but my husband likes to stay home.
2. My husband likes to watch football games on TV, but I hate watching sports.
3. I am an excellent dancer, but my husband doesn't dance well at all.
4. I want to have a large family, but my husband doesn't want any children.
5. My husband is a nice person, but we have a lot of problems.

Combining Sentences (p. 102)

1. My husband and I have to settle our differences, or I will leave him.
2. He will talk with me about our problems, or we will have to see a marriage counselor.
3. He has to do something, or I will divorce him.
4. He will have to change, or I will leave him.
5. He will make some changes, or I will make some changes for him.

Combining Sentences (p. 103)

1. Life has its downs, but it also has its ups.
2. I have to work very hard, or my family would not have very much.
3. My wife helps us a lot, and our children work after school.
4. Together we do well, but it is very hard.
5. One day our ship will come in, but I don't think it will come very soon.

Direct Quotations (pp. 104–105)

1. Yukio asked, "Why are you going there?"
2. Trevor asked, "Which way should we go?"
3. Betty asked, "How old is she?"
4. Nicholas asked, "What is the name of our new boss?"
5. Carol asked, "How much did you pay for that?"
6. Marta asked, "What is the best way to do this?"
7. Henry asked, "Who made her cry?"
8. George asked, "Why can't I go there tomorrow?"
9. Barbara asked, "Which person is going to jail?"
10. Ken asked, "How can we finish that by tomorrow?"

Direct and Indirect Quotations (p. 106)

1. She said that she does not want to stay here.
2. He said that Jaime was promoted yesterday.
3. Joseph said that we need to know more about that.
4. Benito said that Jane is going to visit her sister today.
5. Paul said that his best friend is getting married tomorrow.

End Marks (Punctuation) (p. 107)

1. Sharon asked why he didn't go to the store.
2. My brother asked where to meet us.
3. Kimiko asked what we were going to wear later.
4. Does she say that she can come with us?
5. What did she want?
6. Dara asked why we weren't ready yet.
7. Monique asked what was happening at work.
8. Is she still going with your brother?
9. She asked if she could help us.
10. Does Juan care much for his family?

The Pronouns Who, Whom, and Whose (p. 108)

1. Whose	5. Whose	8. Who
2. whom	6. whom	9. Whose
3. Who	7. Who	10. Who
4. whom		

Using the Words Has and Have with Verbs (p. 109)

1. went	6. has known
2. have run	7. has grown
3. caught	8. took
4. drank	9. began
5. have gotten	10. ran

Adding ing to Verbs with a Helping Verb (p. 110)

1. is writing	6. is going
2. are building	7. is growing
3. are waiting	8. are telling
4. are staying	9. is crying
5. is doing	10. are drying

The Verb Be (p. 111)

1. have been	5. has been	8. was
2. have been	6. were	9. has been
3. were	7. was	10. has been
4. was		

The Verbs Forget, Forgets, Forgot, Will Forget, and Forgotten (p. 112)

1. forgot	5. forgotten	8. forgotten
2. will forget	6. forgot	9. forget
3. forgotten	7. forgotten	10. will forget
4. forgot		

Spelling (p. 113)

Sample answers:
1. (vegetables) Peas and carrots are my favorite vegetables.
2. (marriage) I believe in marriage.
3. (written) Sharon has written a lot about that.
4. (Thursday) We will meet on Thursday.
5. (sincerely) They are sincerely sorry about that.

Alphabetizing (Using the Dictionary) (p. 114)

1. No	3. Yes	5. Yes	7. Yes	9. Yes
2. Yes	4. No	6. No	8. Yes	10. No

Chapter Five Review
Capitalizing (Common Nouns and Proper Nouns) (p. 115)

1. C	6. Carnegie Center
2. Mexico	7. C
3. Aunt Kim	8. Chinese
4. March	9. C
5. C	10. C

Combining Sentences (p. 115)

1. The show was funny, but we didn't like it.
2. I enjoy watching television, but the commercials bother me.
3. My fiancé is not very popular, but I like him, anyway.
4. Fred's husband saw the attacker, but his wife didn't want him to go to the police.
5. Many persons saw the attacker, but they did nothing about him.

Combining Sentences (p. 116)

1. Do it now, or we will have difficulty later on.
2. She will continue to go to school, or her parents will not support her.
3. You have to work harder, or your boss will probably fire you.
4. Eat your vegetables now, or I will not give you any dessert.
5. Frank needs to exercise more, or he will get much fatter.

Combining Sentences (pp. 116–117)

1. That was the hardest thing to do, but I had to do it.
2. No one said anything, but we knew everything.
3. We opened a window, and a bird flew in.
4. Seth jogs every morning, and his wife swims every afternoon.
5. Write down everything, or we will forget to buy something.

Direct Quotations (p. 117)

1. Herbert asked, "Why are you doing that?"
2. Florence asked, "Who is going to the party tomorrow?"
3. I asked, "What are you doing later?"
4. Mateo asked, "Is that the truth?"
5. Julia asked, "Did you do that?"

Direct and Indirect Quotations (p. 117)

1. Berta said that she needs more time to do that.
2. Jane said that she is happy about this.
3. Maria said that David has everything he needs.
4. Laurent said that Tara is a lovely young woman.
5. Larry said that he likes working here.

End Marks (Punctuation) (p. 118)

1. Are you really going to do that?
2. He asked whether you were going to do that.
3. I asked him if he knew what time it was.
4. How late are you?
5. Did you ask if he will attend the meeting?

The Pronouns *Who*, *Whom*, and *Whose* (p. 118)

1. whom
2. Whose
3. whom
4. Who
5. whom

Using the Words *Has* and *Have* with Verbs (p. 118)

1. have gone
2. has helped
3. has met
4. have known
5. bit

Adding *ing* to Verbs with a Helping Verb (pp. 118–119)

1. is writing
2. are going
3. are staying
4. are playing
5. is driving

The Verb *Be* (p. 119)

1. have been
2. were
3. has been
4. have been
5. was

The Verbs *Forget*, *Forgets*, *Forgot*, *Will Forget*, and *Forgotten* (p. 119)

1. forgot
2. forgotten
3. will forget
4. forgets
5. forgot

Spelling (p. 119)

Sample answers:
1. Vegetables are good for you.
2. More young people are interested in marriage now.
3. Have you written to your parents yet?
4. I like Thursday because it's close to Friday.
5. He seems to act sincerely.

Alphabetizing (Using the Dictionary) (p. 120)

1. No   2. Yes   3. No   4. No   5. No

Posttest
Capitalizing (p. 123)

1. C
2. Lincoln Center
3. Marshal Company
4. C
5. Aunt Sharon
6. General Grant
7. C
8. C
9. C
10. C

Singular and Plural Subjects (p. 123)

You should have a line under the following.
1. teacher (S)
2. noise (S)
3. problems (P)
4. boyfriends (P)
5. parents (P)

Agreement of Subject and Verb (p. 123)

You should have a line under the following.
1. is
2. are
3. comes
4. drives
5. protect

Combining Sentences (p. 124)

1. Luis, Jane, and Claire have their own bowling balls.
2. Gregorio, Hiro, and Choi want their own cars now.
3. Roberto, Pierre, and Mary want their own businesses soon.
4. Georgio, Judit, and Keung have changed their minds again.
5. Tim, James, and Diane are still looking for their dream mates.

Combining Sentences (p. 125)

1. Life is more difficult today, but it is also more exciting.
2. Some of my friends finished school, and they have good jobs.
3. I dropped out of school, and now no one will hire me.
4. I have to do something with my life, but it is hard to know what to do.
5. I must get a decent job, or my wife will leave me.

Combining Sentences (p. 125)

1. C
2. Everyone is very helpful, and they want me to get ahead.
3. My wife is supporting me, and she wants me to do well.
4. C
5. We are in this together, and we will make it.

Direct Quotations (p. 126)

1. Jeff's friend asked, "Is it time to go yet?"
2. Maria asked, "Why does this coat cost so much?"
3. José said, "Everything seems to cost a lot."
4. Joseph said, "That person looks odd."
5. Paula asked, "Did the police catch the robber?"

Direct and Indirect Quotations (p. 126)

1. Franco said that he needs more time to finish the work.
2. Luisa said that this has been a good year for her.
3. Mei said that the storekeeper charged her too much.
4. Harry said that his children need many things.
5. Anthony said that Jerry is his best friend.

The Pronouns *Anybody, Anyone, Everybody, Everyone, Nobody, No One, Somebody,* and *Someone* (p. 127)

You should have a line under the following.
1. is
2. is
3. needs
4. has
5. cries

Pronouns (Showing Ownership or Belonging To) (p. 127)

1. hers; her
2. His
3. Its
4. Their
5. theirs; their

Pronouns and What They Refer To (p. 127)

1. its
2. his
3. their
4. her
5. their

The Pronouns *Who, Whom,* and *Whose* (p. 128)

1. whom
2. Who
3. whom
4. Whose
5. Who

End Marks (Punctuation) (p. 128)

1. They asked when we arrived yesterday.
2. James said he knows about Gil and Elena.
3. Who refused the invitation?
4. She asked if they could stay a little longer.
5. This is an incredible view.
   or: This is an incredible view!

Adjectives (p. 128)

1. best
2. more
3. good
4. better
5. worse

Regular and Irregular Verbs (p. 128)

1. stayed
2. tried
3. cleaned
4. seemed
5. walked
6. forgot
7. went
8. took
9. ran
10. did

The Verbs *Catch*, *Catches*, *Caught*, and *Will Catch* (p. 129)

1. caught
2. catch
3. will catch
4. catches
5. will catch

Using the Words *Has* and *Have* with Verbs (p. 129)

1. have fished
2. have been
3. saw
4. opened
5. has worked

Adding *ing* to Verbs with a Helping Verb (p. 129)

1. is making
2. is running
3. is working
4. are living
5. are trying

The Verb *Be* (p. 130)

1. is
2. are
3. has been
4. was
5. will be

The Verbs *Forget*, *Forgets*, *Forgot*, *Will Forget*, and *Forgotten* (p. 130)

1. forgot
2. have forgotten
3. have forgotten
4. will forget
5. forget

Adverbs (p. 130)

1. faster
2. most steadily
3. more sure
4. more carefully
5. more quietly

The Words *Well*, *Better*, and *Best* (p. 130)

1. best
2. well
3. best
4. better
5. well

Showing Ownership or Belonging To (p. 131)

1. fox's
2. James's
3. shelves'
4. mice's
5. knife's
6. class's
7. wolf's
8. girls'
9. shirt's
10. children's

The Comma (p. 131)

1. NC
2. NC
3. NC
4. At the shelter there were tired, hungry people.
5. I love this soft, fluffy blanket.

Contractions (p. 131)

1. He is; she has
2. I will; he is
3. I am; we are
4. It is; they have
5. He will; you are

The Words *A* or *An* (p. 132)

1. an elevator
2. an odor
3. a hospital
4. a year
5. an hour
6. a home
7. an uncle
8. a family
9. a union card
10. an honest person

Writing an Invitation (p. 132)

Sample letter:

> February 1, 1990
>
> Dear Donato,
>
> David and I are giving an anniversary party for Felix and Diana on Saturday, February 14. The party will be at Felix's house at 8:30 P.M. Each of us is bringing something special to the party. Please phone me by January 9 so that I can give you all the details. My phone number is 555-9611.
>
> Your friend,
> Sharon Brown

Writing a Business Letter (p. 133)

Sample letter:

> 1457 Broad Street
> Los Angeles, California 91351
> September 4, 1990
>
> Frank Galillio
> Galillio's Restaurant
> 214 Derby Street
> Los Angeles, California 91354
>
> Dear Mr. Galillio:
>
> I am answering your ad in yesterday's Los Angeles Times for a short-order cook. I need a new job because I have just moved to this area. I have been a short-order cook for ten years and have good references. I am fast, dependable, honest, hardworking, and healthy.
>
> I look forward to hearing from you. My home phone number is 555-5390.
>
> Sincerely yours,
> Adolfo Díaz

Spelling (p. 134)

1. until	11. favorite
2. holiday	12. please
3. Thanksgiving	13. quiet
4. loose	14. excellent
5. enough	15. beginning
6. niece	16. turkey
7. science	17. sentence
8. sincerely	18. marriage
9. written	19. Thursday
10. finally	20. vegetables

Alphabetizing (Using the Phone Book) (p. 134)

1. No   2. Yes   3. Yes   4. No   5. Yes